Skyline 5

Student's Book

Simon Brewster

Paul Davies

Mickey Rogers

MACMILLAN

Contents

Functions	Vocabulary	Pronunciation
• Talking about events in the past • Giving personal opinions on music and art • Talking and writing about famous people • Talking about conferences	• Strategies for understanding words • Words that go together	• Word stress – different parts of speech
• Talking about technology now and in the future • Talking about genetics • Doing a technology survey	• Multi-word verb meanings	• Stress with separable two-word verbs
• Talking about imitation products • Talking about food and food festivals • Discussing the movie industry • Making a business plan	• Food • Business language	• Sounds – /eɪ/, /eə/ and /aɪ/
• Talking about events in or around the present • Describing character • Discussing beliefs, relationships and communication • Preparing for a foreign exchange	• Suffixes: *-able*, *-ate*, *-ful*, *-ible* • Words for gesture, posture and voice	
• Discussing past and present youth culture • Talking about cities now and in the past • Putting a case for a new UNESCO site	• Recording vocabulary • City-related words past and present	
• Talking about science fiction • Talking about personal plans for the future • Negotiating to choose members of a team • Planning a community project	• Synonyms • The environment • The language of presentation	• Intonation – showing interest

Contents

Songsheets

Irregular verbs
Pronunciation chart

Functions

- Talking about the business of sport
- Describing different parts of the body
- Talking about injuries to the body
- Analyzing the Olympic Games

- Describing the face
- Giving advice
- Talking about past processes and events
- Promoting new products

- Discussing superstitions
- Talking about attitudes to life
- Talking about cause and effect

- Expressing opinions
- Talking about past traditions
- Discussing how sociable you are and analyzing personality

- Describing people by comparing them with something
- Talking about the science and ethics of cloning
- Talking about future hopes and expressing regret
- Discussing the treatment of and the uses of animals

and activities

- Making inferences
- Writing a letter
- Listening for the general idea
- Explain this!

Vocabulary

- The body and sports
- Business and money

- The human face
- Medicine
- Commercials

- Affixes
- Flying
- Career planning

- Opinion and (dis)agreement
- Words relating to coffee growing and drinking

- Similes
- Animals

- Working out meaning

- Listening for detail
- Chain story

Pronunciation

- Weak form of *that* in relative clauses

- Intonation – questions

- Intonation – lists

- Sounds – homophones

- Weak forms and linking

- Listening for inference
- Educated guesses

Unit 1 The 20th century

1 Culture

1 Speaking, writing and reading

a We are now in a new millennium: the 20th century is suddenly recent history. Write your favorites from 20th century popular culture, from your own or other countries, in the table below.

My two favorite 20th century ...	First choice	Second choice
actors or actresses		
songs or pieces of music		
singers or bands		
TV drama programs		
TV comedy programs		

b In groups, compare your choices. How many are from English-speaking countries and how many are from your country? Does that suggest anything about popular culture, or about you?

c Given their choices, what do you think the students in your group are like? Write about each one.

Maria seems to be serious (romantic / a bit wild ...). *I think she is interested in politics* (has a good sense of humor / likes excitement ...). *She probably ...*

d Read and discuss people's comments. Do you agree with the descriptions of you?

2 Speaking and listening

a Match four of these people with the works of art. In pairs, discuss your answers and what you know and think about these artists and their work.

1 Pablo Picasso
2 Charlie Chaplin
3 Vivian Leigh and Clark Gable
4 Elvis Presley
5 Isabel Allende
6 Steven Spielberg

Guernica

The Gold Rush

b Listen to a radio discussion program. What does the man consider to be the two main characteristics of 20th century culture compared with 19th century culture? Compare your answers in pairs.

c Listen again and note the following things.

1 two or three ways that culture entered people's homes in the 20th century

2 the attitude of many musicians and singers towards recording versus live performance

3 why the movies are representative of 20th century culture

3 Pronunciation: word stress

a Listen to part of the program. What do you notice about the word *record*?

b Listen to the pronunciation of the underlined words in A and B. Do the nouns or verbs in these examples have the stress on the first syllable?

	A	B
1	She's going to record that song.	I have a record of that song.
2	They export a lot of movies.	Movies are a major export of the U.S.
3	Some movies insult our intelligence.	Most TV is an insult to our intelligence.
4	Most countries import TV programs.	Latin music is a major import into the U.S.

c Practice saying the sentences, stressing the underlined words correctly.

4 Reading and speaking

a Read these quotes about culture. Beside each one write your reaction: *I agree, I disagree* or *I don't understand.*

3
Culture of the mind must be subservient to the heart.
Mahatma Gandhi, Indian, 1869-1948

2
A man should be just cultured enough to be able to look with suspicion upon culture.
Samuel Butler, English, 1835-1902

1
Culture is to know the best that has been said and thought in the world.
Matthew Arnold, English, 1822-88

4
No culture can live if it attempts to be exclusive.
Mahatma Gandhi, Indian, 1869-1948

5
When I hear anyone talk of culture, I reach for my revolver.
Hermann Goering, German, 1893-1946

6
Culture is everything. Culture is the way we dress, the way we carry our heads, the way we walk, the way we tie our ties – it is not only the fact of writing books or building houses.
Aimé Cesair, Martinique French, contemporary

b Discuss your reactions in groups. Use the quotes you agree with and your ideas to write a paragraph on culture.

2 History and politics

1 Speaking

a Can you identify each of these 20th century scenes? How do you feel about them?

b Match these major 20th century events with dates from the box.

| 1910–17 | 1914–18 | 1917–21 | 1936–39 |
| 1939–45 | ~~1961–73~~ | 1969 | 1989 |

Vietnam War ...._1961–73_........

World War II ....

first humans on the moon ....

World War I ....

fall of the Berlin Wall ....

Mexican Revolution ....

Spanish Civil War ....

Russian Revolution ....

2 Listening and speaking

a Listen to a college history class. What two things (apart from revolutions and wars) does the professor consider extremely significant in the 20th century?

b Read these incomplete class notes. Then listen again and complete them.

c Do you agree with the professor about the most important changes of the 20th century?

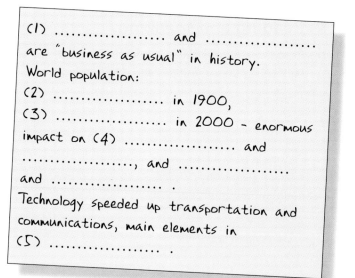

(1) .... and .... are "business as usual" in history. World population:
(2) .... in 1900,
(3) .... in 2000 – enormous impact on (4) .... and ...., and .... and ....
Technology speeded up transportation and communications, main elements in
(5) ....

3 Speaking and reading

a Several advanced countries, including Britain, Japan and Sweden, still have monarchies. What do you know about the British monarchy?

1 Is the present queen the first, second or third Queen Elizabeth?

2 Who is the present heir or heiress to the throne?

3 How many marriages in the Queen's immediate family ended in divorce in the 20th century?

4 Do you think most Britons are for or against the monarchy?

b Read the article and check your answers.

GLORIOUS OR RIDICULOUS?

The British, or at least the English, monarchy is said to have lasted about a thousand years and to have provided enviable political stability. However, England did actually have a revolution, execute its king and establish a republic under Cromwell from 1649 to 1660, long before the French or Russians dreamed of it. Will England abandon the monarchy again in the future and switch to republicanism?

The image of the monarchy certainly changed in the 20th century. In 1936, Edward VIII abdicated, choosing the love of a woman (an American divorcee!) over his inherited duty to the nation. Then, in 1978, Queen Elizabeth II's sister, Princess Margaret, got divorced, breaking a royal rule and creating a small scandal. A decade later, the media were full of gossip about Charles and Di, and Andrew and Fergie. Eventually, both couples divorced (as did their elder sister, Princess Anne) and Prince Charles made his liaison with Camilla Parker Bowles fully public. The Royal Family had become too human. Moreover, the divorce of Prince Charles, the heir to the throne, left serious constitutional questions.

So how did the British feel about their monarchy at the turn of the century? A 1998 poll showed 18% against having a Royal Family, while another poll in 2000 showed an increase to 27%. Many politicians felt the same, and saw the monarchy as an anachronism. One Member of Parliament recently described the monarchy as absurd and expensive, and many echoed him. Such public statements by MPs technically constituted treason, but people felt free to express opinions against the monarchy and for a republic, through reform not revolution. Britain is probably still a long way from becoming a republic, but not half as far as it used to be.

c On the basis of this article and your other knowledge, what is your opinion of the British monarchy?

4 Grammar builder: connectors

a Find the words on the left in the article and underline them. Then match them with the pairs of words or phrases with similar meanings on the right.

1	however	**a)**	as a result, therefore
2	then	**b)**	furthermore, besides
3	eventually	**c)**	next, after that
4	moreover	**d)**	but, in spite of
5	so	**e)**	in the end, finally

b Connectors can have similar meanings, but are used in different grammatical contexts and with different punctuation. Complete these sentences with connectors from the boxes. More than one answer may be possible.

1 **a)** The monarchy survived the 20th century, ... its image suffered.

   b) .... the monarchy's image suffered, it survived the 20th century.

   c) The monarchy's image suffered. ...., it survived the 20th century.

> however   but
> although

2 **a)** .... tradition is strong, republicans are still in a minority.

   b) Tradition is strong, ... republicans are still in a minority.

   c) Tradition is strong. ...., republicans are still in a minority.

> so   therefore
> because

3 Heroes and villains

1 Speaking

In groups, identify these people. Discuss whether each is a hero / heroine, a villain or neither.

2 Speaking and reading

a In pairs, note as many things as you can about Nelson Mandela, e.g.

- his nationality
- the reason for his political struggle
- the length of his imprisonment
- why he shared the Nobel Peace Prize with another man
- his racial philosophy

b Read the brief biography and check your ideas.

Nelson Rolihlahla Mandela, South Africa's first black President, was born in 1918 into the royal family of the Tembu
5 Tribe. Like other black children fortunate enough to get a basic education, he went to a British missionary school. While he was studying at Fort Hare University,
10 he organized a boycott and was expelled. He eventually obtained a law degree from the University of South Africa and set up South Africa's first black law firm with
15 Oliver Tambo.

In 1944, Walter Sisulu, Mandela and Tambo formed the African National Congress Youth League to fight more actively for black rights
20 than the old ANC did. Mandela was continually arrested during the late 1950s and eventually tried for treason in 1961. When the trial ended with his acquittal, he
25 formed the ANC's military wing, Umkhonto we Sizwe (Spear of the Nation). He was arrested again and sentenced in 1964 to life in prison for sabotage and attempting to
30 overthrow the government. Mandela spent the next 27 years in prison, but managed to maintain contact with the ANC and remain its leading figure.
35 Slowly, the government began to realize it would be impossible for the white minority to continue dominating the black majority through "apartheid" indefinitely,
40 and Mandela met with President P.W. Botha in July 1989 and his successor, President F.W. de Klerk, in December that year. Mandela was released in 1990.
45 After he had consulted with the ANC leadership, Mandela went on a world tour to persuade Western leaders to maintain economic sanctions against South Africa and
50 to raise funds to help the ANC function as a political party. Negotiations with the ruling National Party led to the ANC's decision to suspend its armed
55 struggle after nearly 30 years, and then to agreements on an interim government with both parties as partners for five years. Further talks in 1993 led to the
60 establishment of a majority-rule constitution. In December that year, Mandela and de Klerk received Nobel Peace Prizes for their promotion of democracy in
65 South Africa.

In 1994, the ANC won the country's first all-race elections and Mandela became President. He consistently urged reconciliation
70 between the races, in spite of his long struggle under white dictatorship. His efforts at reconciliation culminated in May 1995 with the approval of a new
75 South African constitution that prohibited discrimination against the country's minorities, including whites. He retired in 1999, having achieved his goal.

c An important skill in reading is inferring meaning or "reading between the lines". Check your ability to do this by answering these questions.

1 Did white children attend Mandela's school?

2 Why was the new Youth League more active than the old ANC?

3 Why was Mandela continually arrested in the 1950s?

4 Why was Mandela an activist for 17 years before turning to violence?

5 Were Botha and de Klerk black or white?

3 Word builder: strategies for understanding words

a Underline the following words and phrases in the biography. How many did you already know? How many did you guess, e.g. from similarity to your language or from context? How many are you still uncertain about?

1 expel (line 11)

2 set up (line 13)

3 Youth League (line 18)

4 treason (line 23)

5 acquittal (line 24)

6 overthrow (line 30)

7 apartheid (line 39)

8 release (line 44)

9 raise funds (line 50)

10 armed struggle (line 54–55)

11 further (line 58)

12 approval (line 74)

b Check the words you aren't sure of in a dictionary. What information about the meaning or use of the words is new for you?

> **Learning tip**
>
> Make vocabulary learning a high priority: it is **very** important. Try to remember words that go together:
> He was expelled from ... the university.
> He set up ... a law firm.
> He attempted to overthrow ... the government.
> He was released from ... prison.
> Which words from exercise 3a would you want to learn?

4 Grammar builder: past time clauses

a Complete the sentences with appropriate verb structures.

1 While he .... (study) at Fort Hare University, he .... (organize) a boycott.

2 When the trial .... (end), he .... (form) the ANC's military wing.

3 He .... (follow) political events all the time while he .... (serve) his long prison sentence.

4 After he .... (consult) with the ANC leadership, he .... (go) on a world tour.

b Check in pairs. Why have you used past simple, past progressive or past perfect in each case? Are there sometimes different options? Would you use similar structures in your language?

5 Speaking

In groups, propose and discuss your own candidates for 20th century heroes / heroines or villains.

LANGUAGE for life:
conference-*going*

---

① Conferences, conventions, congresses ...

Whatever they're called, professional gatherings, often in good hotels in attractive cities or resorts, became a part of many people's working lives in the last half of the 20th century. The reasons why people attend them vary: as speakers or exhibitors, for professional updating and development, as a reward for good work, to escape from routine work. Whatever their reason for attending, most conference-goers manage to combine some pleasure with business.

How do you think the people in each of the scenes on page 13 are spending their time? How would you be spending your time? Have you, or has anyone you know, attended any conferences? When, where, why? What was most and least enjoyable about them?

---

② Following the program

Here are two abstracts from a conference program. Which talk would you go to? Why?

SATURDAY 21	9:15-10:45 a.m.

SECONDARY EDUCATION BY TELEVISION

This talk will look at how secondary education is provided via television to isolated or under-resourced communities in several different countries. In South Africa this includes rural and poor urban communities. First, systems will be described and samples of television material shown. Then the advantages and disadvantages of different systems will be discussed. Finally, a conclusion will be drawn – that each system should suit the situation in which it is used.

Nancy Matutu is an educational television producer in South Africa.

Room 2

BAROCK AROUND THE CLOCK

Some programs that combine classical and contemporary popular music, e.g. baroque and rock, in imaginative ways have proved very attractive to the general public, including young viewers. However, not all programs of this kind work well. This talk will analyze examples of what has been especially successful in the Netherlands and what has not. Selection, presentation, scheduling and promotion are all very important.

Ed van Dijk and Neelie Ruding are editors of a music magazine in the Netherlands.

Room 5

Public announcements are often difficult to understand. Although they should be clear enough at a conference, a little practice can do no harm.

Listen to an announcement at the start of the Saturday session of the conference about changes to the program. Note the changes in your program.

③ Making a contribution

Here are some possible topics for talks at this conference (7th Convention of Cultural and Educational Television). Are you particularly interested in any of these topics? Why? Why not?

- Negative television: bad role models, violence, humiliating games, etc.
- Documentaries: education and entertainment combined
- Local culture versus Americanized globalization
- Classic movies: a vast source of high-quality material
- Exporting culture: presenting marketable aspects of your country's culture to the world

You've probably never given a talk at a conference, but you may one day – and perhaps even in English (most international conferences use English). So once again, a little practice can do no harm.

- Find two or three people interested in the same topic as you – one of those listed, or one you think of.
- Brainstorm ideas for the talk and make notes.
- Write an abstract of about 100 words – topic, main aspects to be presented, general conclusion.
- Give the talk a title.
- Put your abstract on the board with other groups' abstracts to form a conference program.

Read the abstracts and decide on two talks you would be interested in giving.

④ Party night

No conference is complete without a party. It's the ideal opportunity to meet new people and at an international conference that means people from other countries. Which of the people in the pictures above would you like to talk to at this party? Why?

Now imagine you're someone in television or education from another country. Decide:

- the country you are from
- your name
- your age, marital status, etc.
- your specific work (e.g. teacher, TV director, writer, educational psychologist)
- your travel plans (the conference is in Switzerland – are you going straight home afterwards, or are you going to travel around Europe a bit?)

Then ... join the party!

Unit 2 People and technology

Laura

Marsha

1 Living with machines

1 Speaking

a What are the differences between Marsha and Laura's lifestyles? Which is more like yours?

b Which of the following are, or soon will be: essential (1), useful (2) or unnecessary (3) for you? Write 1, 2 or 3.

transportation	car	○	bus	○		
	train	○	plane	○		
communication	cell phone	○	home phone	○		
	public phone	○	WAP phone	○	home computer	○
	laptop	○	palmtop	○	Internet café	○
domestic appliances	microwave	○	dishwasher	○	washing machine	○
entertainment	walkman	○	stereo	○	television	○
	VCR	○	movie theater	○	DVD player	○

2 Speaking and reading

a Which of the following features do you expect to find in many cars by 2050?

non-gasoline engine ○
crash prevention radar ○
top speed of 300 kph ○
ability to fly ○
automatic pilot ○
computer joystick for steering ○

b Read the article opposite and check (✔) which features above are mentioned.

c Read the article again and answer these questions.

1 Where does the electricity for the house and car come from?
2 What does the car have instead of a steering wheel and pedals?
3 Why is it almost impossible to crash the car?
4 What happens if the driver becomes sleepy?
5 How can the car reach a destination if the driver is sleeping?
6 Which features have already been tried out?

DRIVEN BY CARS

It's 2050 and one American passion has withstood the test of time: we like to drive. You decide to hit the road. First, you unplug your car from your house. That's right – your car's fuel cells (those hydrogen-powered devices) turn out enough electricity for your home and your car.

You settle into the driver's seat and grasp the joystick (steering wheels and pedals are history). All movements of the car – accelerating, turning, braking – are controlled by a joystick familiar to anyone brought up on computer games. You drive in traffic with absolute confidence. Your car is programmed with radar to sense a crash before it happens and activate the brakes.

An alarm sounds. The sensor in the instrument panel has checked the pupils of your eyes and decided you are getting sleepy. You pull over into the "sleep lane". You lay a course on your satellite-guided navigation system, switch the autopilot on and climb into the back seat for a sleep. The car, reading computer chips in the road, takes over the driving.

This is not science fiction. Automakers are spending billions researching all these futuristic features. General Motors has tried out an "intelligent highway" in California that allows cars to drive on autopilot. Daimler Chrysler fits prototype cars with joysticks and many drivers operate them better than steering wheels. Every carmaker is rushing to replace the internal combustion engine with fuel cells. Satellite navigation systems are already on the road. Soon your car will be driving you.

3 Word builder: multi-word verb meanings

a Match the following multi-word verbs from the article with the words or phrases on the right.

1 turn out (electricity)	a) raise
2 bring up (children on computer games)	b) move to the side
3 pull over (into the "sleep lane")	c) test
4 take over (the driving)	d) produce
5 try out (an "intelligent highway")	e) take charge of

b Replace the verbs in *italic* with appropriate forms of the multi-word verbs in the box. Use a dictionary, but only when necessary.

Randolph Kenny (1) *started* flying at 70. After he retired, he bought a ranch and (2) *found* an old Cessna in a field. A mechanic helped him fix it up. Then a friend who had been a pilot in the U.S. Air Force came to stay and (3) *tested* the plane. It was fine. Randolph went up with him and (4) *took charge of* the controls several times.

> come across   keep on   get over
> get to   give up   put up with
> set out   take off   take over
> take up   turn out   try out

In the following week he learned how to (5) *leave the ground* and land. He (6) *proved* to be a natural at flying. After his friend left, he (7) *continued* practicing daily. Then he had a mild heart attack and did not fly for a time. But once he had (8) *recovered from* the problem, he was back in the air.

One day he decided to fly to his pilot friend's ranch 200 miles away. He (9) *left* early one morning, but he got lost in the clouds and his chest began to hurt. He (10) *tolerated* the pain, found his way out of the clouds and managed to (11) *reach* his own ranch again. He (12) *stopped* flying that day.

4 Speaking and listening

a In which situations can a cell phone be a big help or a big nuisance?

b Listen to a short scene from a situation. In groups, decide where it is and what happened.

c Do you know of any stories connected with cell phones?

2 Genetic engineering

1 Speaking

We can now genetically modify plants and animals, and clone animals to get two or more identical ones. In theory, we can do the same with humans. Discuss these questions in pairs.

1 Would you prefer to "design" your children (determine their height, hair and eye color, intelligence, etc.) or accept the lottery of nature? Why?

2 Would you like to have a cloned copy of yourself? How might a clone be useful and how might "it" be a problem?

2 Reading and speaking

a Read the article and find the following.

- a definition of the human genome
- the relationship between genes and DNA
- the length of the human genome document

THE BEGINNING OF REAL BIOLOGY

On June 26 2000, Francis Collins, head of the Human Genome Project, and Craig Venter, head of Celera Genomics, jointly announced that they had completed the reading of a "rough draft" of the human genome – the complete set of human DNA. This was the beginning of a whole new way of understanding human biology. Whatever we discover from the genome about how our bodies work, it will be infinitely more than everything we knew before.

It was also the end to a great detective story. In 1860, Gregor Mendel made the unexpected discovery that inheritance comes in tiny particles called genes. In 1953, James Watson and Francis Crick made the even more unexpected discovery that those particles are digital messages written along strands of DNA in a four-letter chemical code. In 1961, Marshall Nirenberg and

Johann Matthaei cracked the first "word" in that code, revealing how DNA instructs the cell to build proteins. It was then inevitable that one day we would read all the genetic messages that a human body inherits.

Of course, the genome announcement was just a beginning, for the document that was produced – as long as 900 bibles – was almost entirely mysterious. Whoever makes sense of large parts of it will become famous. We stand on the shore of a continent of new knowledge.

But most people simply hoped it would help cure cancer and speculated about customized medicine, with drugs designed for the individual, not the population. Or they worried that it would lead to designer babies for the rich and feared that medical insurance might not be given to people known to have high medical risks.

b Read the article again and answer these questions.

1 When was the first version of the human genome completed?

2 What was Mendel's great discovery?

3 Why didn't the human genome have immediate applications after it was "read"?

4 What are the possible benefits and dangers from our knowledge of the human genome?

c In groups, discuss whether you feel more optimistic or more pessimistic about these developing discoveries.

3 Grammar builder: *whoever, whatever, whenever, wherever*

a Complete these sentences with *whoever, whatever, whenever* or *wherever*.

1 I feel absolutely amazed .... , I read about modern science and technology.

2 .... makes sense of the genome will become famous.

3 Genetically modified crops can't be a bad thing, ... some ecologists say.

4 .... you go in the U.S. nowadays there are GM crops.

b Complete these sentences with your own ideas. Then compare them in groups.

1 Whenever ...., I feel really happy.

2 Whoever thought of .... was a genius.

3 I always take .... wherever I go.

4 Whatever you do, never ....

5 I will eternally admire whoever ....

6 Whenever I feel stressed, I ....

> **Language assistant**
> These *wh-ever* words mean "It does not matter who / what / when / where."

4 Listening

a The most general application of genetic engineering at present is to plants. Listen to two farmers talking about GM crops. Who is more positive about them and who is more negative, Fred or Jack?

b Listen again and complete these notes.

WHITFIELD FARM
The Best in GM Crops
Science in the Field

Advantages of GM crops	They repel (1) ...., resist (2) ...., and are more (3) .... They are what the (4) .... wants.
Disadvantage of GM crops	They can be very (5) .... to new (6) .... of pest or disease.

5 Writing, reading and speaking

a Draw a line down the middle of the page in your notebook. At the top of the left-hand column write "Leave nature alone" and at the top of the right-hand column write "Human progress". In groups, write two or more ideas for each side.

If we destroy nature, we destroy ourselves.

With genetic engineering we might eliminate cancer.

Your teacher will put your ideas on the board.

b Read and discuss the ideas. Then vote for or against the free development of genetic engineering.

c In pairs, use the notes on the board to develop two paragraphs about genetic engineering: one for and one against.

3 Technology dependence and risks

1 Speaking

a List all the electrical or electronic devices you switched on yesterday, e.g. the light, the hairdryer, the radio, the microwave oven.

b In groups, compare and discuss your lists. How dependent are you on electrical and electronic devices? Which could you manage without and which are you completely dependent on?

2 Grammar builder: word order with two-word verbs

a Write the verbs in the box on the appropriate line below. Look words up in a dictionary if necessary. The example will help you.

> come across (an old photograph)   fix up (a machine)
> get over (an illness)   look for (a book)   look up (a word)
> put on (a hat)   run into (a friend)   stand for (a term)
> switch/turn off (the light)   take after (your mother)
> take over (a job)   try out (a car)

Non-separable: come across,

Separable: fix up,

Language assistant

Some two-word verbs with objects are separable: She **switched off** the radio or She **switched** the radio **off**. Others are not: She **looked for** the **magazine** (not She **looked** the magazine **for**). Other two-word verbs do not have an object: The light **went off**.

b Look at these sentences. Where do we put the pronoun object (e.g. *me*, *him*, *it*, *them*) of a separable verb?

*She switched on the lights when she arrived. When she left she forgot to switch **them** off.*

*He turned down his stereo when we complained, but he soon turned **it** up again.*

What happens with the object of a non-separable verb?

*I ran into an old friend yesterday. I ran into **her** in the library.*

c Write the words and phrases in an appropriate order.

1 in a field / across / an old plane / came / he
2 up / a mechanic / helped / him / it / fix
3 was / adventurous / his father / and / he / after / him / took
4 out / a pilot friend / the plane / tried
5 stands / the acronym / "save our souls" / for / SOS

> **Learning tip**
>
> Learn vocabulary (including multi-word verbs) by using it. Look for or create opportunities to use new words you think could be important for you. That will make the vocabulary active (you can use it when speaking or writing), not just passive (you just understand it when listening or reading). Check through this lesson and list new words that you would like to have in your active vocabulary. Try to use them (even if only thinking in English) during the next few days.

3 Pronunciation: stress with separable two-word verbs

a Listen to these sentences. Notice that noun objects are frequently stressed, but with pronoun objects, the adverb particle (e.g. *on*, *off*) is usually stressed.

1 She turned the **lights** on. When she left, she forgot to turn them **off**.
2 A noise woke me **up**. It was my wife putting the **cat** out.

b Practice saying the sentences in exercise 3a and these sentences. Underline the stressed words, then listen and check.

1 I asked him to turn the volume down. Later he turned it up again.
2 Why don't you try the job out? If you're OK, you could take it over next month.

4 Speaking, listening and writing

a Look at the photograph of New York one night in 1977. What do you think is happening? Why?

b Listen to the news item and check your ideas. What other problems do you think there were, for example in hospitals?

c In groups, choose one of the following scenarios for technology-related problems that could have enormous consequences. Prepare a presentation on the probability of the problem actually occurring and the possible consequences. Give your presentations group by group.

- Collapse of the Internet, e.g. because of a powerful virus or technical problems like those expected at the beginning of the year 2000.
- An extended traffic and factory shut-down in a major city because of massive air pollution.
- The explosion of an atomic power plant.

LANGUAGE for life:
technology *surveys*

1 How would superheroes manage nowadays?

Could Superheroes wash their clothes in a multi-function washing machine or install a new computer program?

Can you? In this brave new world of ours we continually have to deal with basic and advanced technology.

Check how technologically competent you are or could be by answering this questionnaire.

Compare your score with some classmates. Who is the most and least technologically competent? Do those of you with low technological competence have other abilities or qualities? Perhaps you are artistic (e.g. music, painting, writing, cooking, sewing) or you are sociable (e.g. conversation, jokes, sports, dancing)?

Could you ...	Yes, now	No, never	Maybe, with training
1 ... change an electric fuse?			
2 ... change the tire of a car?			
3 ... program a washing machine?			
4 ... write a document on a computer and print it out?			
5 ... download a program from the Internet?			
6 ... program a VCR to record a program while you are out?			

Scoring: "Yes, now" = 3 points   "No, never" = 0 points   "Maybe, with training" = 1 point

11–18 points: Well done! You're a technological wizard!   5–10 points: You'll be OK with a little help.

0–4 points: Oh dear! How do you cope in this technical world?

② Technology spread

The development and use of technology has been accelerating for a long time. Here are figures for the time it took new technologies to reach 50 million users.

- *radio: 38 years*
- *television:13 years*
- *personal computers: 16 years*
- *World Wide Web: 4 years*

Note: the extra three years for personal computers compared with television was because of the higher cost of the equipment and the greater skill needed to operate it.

Why do you think the mass use of technology is accelerating? How do you feel about this acceleration?

The technological divide between different countries is enormous. Here are figures for the number of people with Internet access by region.

- *Canada / USA: 97 million*
- *Europe: 40.1 million*
- *Asia / Pacific: 27 million*
- *Latin America: 5.3 million*
- *Africa: 1.1 million*

Do you think your country is at the top, in the middle or at the bottom with respect to Internet access and information technology in general? Try listing some things that can be done to catch up with the top countries; consider what can be done in schools first.

③ Change or die

Some organizations develop continuously. Others stagnate and then struggle to change and survive. What do you think of these company offices? Does this company look like a survivor? Do its offices look like the company offices you know?

Listen to Melanie talking about this company, where she works. Have you experienced anything similar, or heard anyone talk about anything similar?

What about the offices of companies, educational institutions and government agencies in your city or district? Do you know any modern offices like these? Or any "antique" ones like Melanie said Daltons used to have? Do you agree with the statement "Change or die," or do you believe tradition is good even in business, education and government?

④ Situation analysis and proposal

If you were in charge of modernizing an institution, you would need to do it in steps. The first step would probably be to make an analysis of the present situation: the good aspects (if any) and bad aspects. Then you would have to consider the needs of the institution, the resources available, and so on, and make a proposal for change, i.e. things you would keep and things you would change.

Just for practice (in case you actually face this situation one day!), think of an institution you know that needs modernizing and write a brief situation analysis and proposal for changes. Remember the steps:

1 *Good aspects (e.g. The offices have lots of space and light. They ...)*
2 *Bad aspects (e.g. The furniture and equipment is very old. Some ...)*
3 *Proposed changes (e.g. We should keep the basic layout, but the walls should be painted ...)*

1 Learning check

1 Progress check

a Complete the conversation. Choose the correct word.

Joe: Hi, Sally. How are you?

Sally: Not so great. (1) *While / Although* we were on vacation, someone broke into our house. (2) *Whoever / Who* did it, they did a good job – they took almost everything!

Joe: That's terrible! They must have been watching your house before you left. Then (3) *before / as soon as* the house was empty, they broke in.

Sally: Yeah, that's what the police said. If only we hadn't gone away!

Joe: Yes, but on the other hand, it's a good thing you weren't home when the burglars broke in. (4) *Whatever / wherever* you lost, it wasn't as important as your safety.

Sally: That's true. (5) *Anyway / Finally*, we can't change what happened.

b Correct the mistakes in the tenses in these sentences. There is one in each sentence.

6 Thanks for your letter. I had read it while I was waiting for the bus. ....

7 When everybody left the party we were cleaning up the mess. ....

8 As soon as I was seeing the man I called the police. ....

9 I was finishing my job in the bar before going to class. ....

10 After she was receiving the news she called my parents. ....

c Complete the sentences with the correct forms of five of the multi-word verbs in the box. Next to each sentence, indicate whether the verb is separable (S) or non-separable (N).

bring up	take over	take after	give back	get over	stand for	run into	try out

11 Your son looks just like you. He doesn't .... his father at all. ....

12 I've found a great new recipe. Come over tonight and I'll .... (it). ....

13 Last night I .... an old high school friend at a party. It was great to see her! ....

14 Marsha had pneumonia. It took her three weeks to .... (it). ....

15 My parents .... (me) in Texas. ....

2 Proficiency check

a Listen to two people talking about exercise. Mark the sentences T (true) or F (false).

1 The man finds his new program easy. T ◯ F ◯
2 When he tells Kate how often he exercises, she doesn't believe him. T ◯ F ◯
3 His routine consists of ten exercises. T ◯ F ◯
4 The woman gets her exercise through running. T ◯ F ◯
5 She wants to take up slow weight training. T ◯ F ◯

b Read the article and match the topic sentences with the paragraphs.

a) Nowhere are these differences of opinion more marked than in the area of exercise.

b) This turtle-speed exercise routine appears to be the answer to many busy people's dreams.

c) One of the characteristics of modern times is that we don't seem to be able to decide what's good for us and what isn't.

EASY DOES IT – OR DOES IT?

(1) ..... Caffeine is bad for you – but it can relieve migraines. You shouldn't drink alcohol – but a little red wine is good for you. Whenever there are three experts on a subject, there are three different opinions!

(2) ..... In the 70s, running was the rage, giving way to a combination of aerobics and weight training in the 80s. In the 90s, combinations of aerobics and martial arts like Tae-Bo became popular.

The 21st century brought a new trend – super-slow weight training. (3) ..... The workout consists of six exercises, and the whole routine takes twenty minutes once a week! The theory is that when you take fourteen seconds to do each repetition, you push your muscles to their maximum capability. This causes certain physiological changes over several days and, as a result, the recovering muscles burn calories. When you add three pounds of muscle, your body needs an extra 9,000 calories per month to maintain the same body weight! So if you keep your diet the same while you burn more calories, obviously you lose weight. Twenty minutes a week – too good to be true? Maybe. Some professionals in the field think it's all the exercise we need, but others believe the body requires some aerobic activity to maintain a healthy cardiovascular system.

c Choose the best completion (a–c) for each sentence.

1 In the areas of health and fitness:
   a) experts generally agree on what's best.
   b) there are many differences of opinion among experts.
   c) there haven't been many changes recently.

2 At the beginning of the 21st century:
   a) most fitness experts recommended running.
   b) most experts began recommending slow weight training.
   c) slow weight training began to be popular.

3 Slow weight training works through:
   a) frequent exercise sessions.
   b) a wide variety of exercises.
   c) extremely slow repetition of specific exercises.

4 According to some experts, slow training can help you:
   a) tone and strengthen your body.
   b) lose weight.
   c) do both of the above.

Unit 3 Global versus local

1 The real thing

1 Speaking

a Look at the different items. Are there any well-known brand names that you associate with them?

b Can you buy fake versions of these or any other well-known brands in your country? What are the most common fake products and where are they sold?

2 Speaking and reading

a The words on the left appear in the article below. Match the words from the article with their correct meaning on the right. Use a dictionary to help you.

1	fake / counterfeit	a)	trademark
2	trade	b)	income
3	legitimate	c)	commerce
4	revenue	d)	tax
5	brand	e)	honest, legal
6	duty	f)	false

A Cheaper prices make illegal copies attractive for consumers

B Major companies lose billions worldwide because of counterfeit goods

C Sales of fake products reduce government income

b Look at the summaries. Read the article quickly and match one summary to each paragraph.

FAKES – A WORLD OF COPYCATS

1 Every year, criminals make millions of dollars selling fake perfumes, clothes, medicines and computer software. Counterfeit goods account for about 7% of total trade across the globe. And the criminals' gains are other people's losses. Take, for example, governments which are unable to collect revenue from indirect taxes and customs duty on legitimate sales.

2 Over 30% of sales in mainland China are estimated to be counterfeit. In India, fake products account for 10% of the revenue for the entire health sector.

Five out of six Yamaha bikes sold worldwide are not the real thing. Nike, the brand which tells you to "just do it", loses $70 million annually to the menace of fake brands and pirate products. Identical fakes cost Gillette $20 million a year, and Proctor and Gamble loses a staggering $150 million on a twelve-month average in China alone.

3 Sometimes consumers prefer to buy an illegal copy of a video, CD-ROM, cassette or software package because it costs less. In Russia, for example, copies of

Microsoft's Office 2000 program sell for just 1% of the list price. Frequently, however, buyers don't realize they are buying a fake instead of the genuine article.

c   Read the article again and answer the questions.

1   Who are the losers in copycat production?
2   Who are the winners in this situation?
3   Which statistics surprised you the most?

3 Listening

a   Listen to a radio report about a police raid. What did the police suspect Jenkins of?

b   Listen again and complete the police report on the crime.

CRIME REPORT

PERSON CHARGED

Name: .... Jenkins

Sex: ....

Age: ....

Occupation: ....

Town of residence: ....

CRIME

Location: warehouse in ....

Type of crime: conspiracy to supply .... goods

Details of crime: Jenkins made .... at

.... and sold them by ....

and at .... Police confiscated ....

pirate CDs and .... cassettes.

4 Pronunciation: /eɪ/, /eə/, /aɪ/

a   Listen to these words from the report.

raid /eɪ/   fairs /eə/   live /aɪ/

b   Say the words in the box, then write them in the correct column of the chart.

raid	fairs	live

stairs shine mail
rain hair mine buy
time care game

c   Listen and check your answers.

d   Can you add two more words to each column in the chart? The words should only have one syllable!

e   Work with a classmate. Read your new words out loud. He / she writes them in the chart.

5 Speaking

Do you know anyone who has bought a pirate cassette, CD, video, CD-ROM or software package? How common is this in your town / country?

2 International and local food

1 Listening and writing

a Make a list of all the different types of fast food in your country, e.g. hamburgers. Find out which are the two most popular fast foods in your class.

b Listen to a historian talking about the beginnings of fast food. Which four types of fast food does she talk about?

c Listen to the interview again and complete the rest of the table.

Type of fast food	Origin	When	Ingredients
			tomatoes, mozzarella cheese, basil, dough
		1834	
	Holland		
			fish, potatoes, batter

2 Word builder: food

a Look at the list of food items and put them in the correct column in the chart.

chicken   basil   beef   wheat   onion   pomegranates   pepper   peaches   yogurt   carrots   apples
olives   barley   melons   cheese   grapes   pork   garlic   milk   oats   cinnamon   ginger

herbs & spices	fruit	vegetables	cereals	meat & poultry	dairy

b Work in groups and try to answer these questions.

1   Make a list of things a vegan will not eat.
2   What food shouldn't a Muslim or a Jew eat?
3   What fruit and vegetables are in season at the moment in your country?
4   What is your favorite food? Is there any food you cannot eat? If so, what and why not?

3 Reading and writing

a Look at these pictures of food eaten at two festivals. Can you name the items in the pictures? Read the article and check your answers.

Rosh Hashanah, the Jewish New Year

Rosh Hashanah is celebrated in September or October. The festival has many symbolic foods such as challah, an egg-bread which is formed into a ring and represents life, continuous health and happiness in the coming year. Other traditional foods sometimes eaten are sesame seeds (for plenty), dried fruit (for a sweet year) and carrots (the word for carrot in Hebrew is similar to the word for decree, meaning God decrees a good new year). There are also olives (for peace and beauty) and pomegranates (which have the same number of seeds as there are Jewish laws).

The Chinese Moon Festival

This festival takes place in mid-fall. Homes are decorated with paper lanterns and families prepare Moon Festival altars with displays of fruits which are round, such as apples, grapes, melons, peaches and pomegranates. Moon cakes are the most typical food. They are made of flour and filled with nuts, sweet potatoes, eggs, pork and even brandy. The cakes are round as they represent the moon.

b Now read some notes made by two students. They have made the notes in two different ways. What do you like about the two systems? Is there anything you don't like? In small groups, discuss your answers.

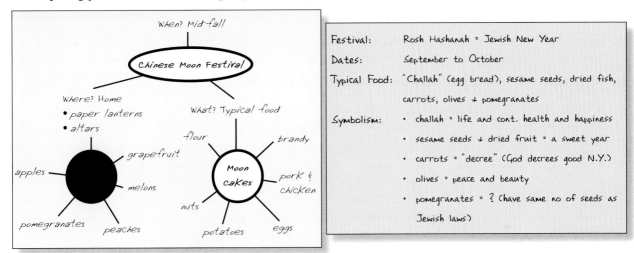

c Unfortunately both students have made mistakes. Look at each set of notes again and find the mistakes. There are three in each set of notes.

4 Grammar builder: nouns in groups

a Look at these examples of nouns in groups. What are the main differences between the two sets of nouns?

1 the girl's leg   lamb's wool   Matthew's book
2 a coffee cup   leather goods   the office reception

b Write at least one more example for each category in exercise 4a.

5 Writing

a Decide which of the note-taking systems from exercise 3b you prefer and make notes about a festival you know where food has symbolic meaning. Include details of the type of festival, dates, decorations, food and drink and any other typical aspects.

b Use your notes to write a short description of the festival.

> **Language assistant**
>
> Noun + 's + noun is normally used only with people and animals: *the boy's shoe, the dog's tail*. Noun + noun is normally used with things, places, materials / ingredients and ideas: *the car door, the hotel lobby, a plastic bag, a history book*.

3 Hollywood versus Bollywood

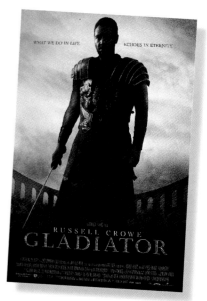

1 Speaking

a Class survey. Write down the names of the last five movies you saw. Discuss them with the class. How many were American and how many were made in your country or other countries?

b Why do you think Hollywood is so powerful in the international movie market?

2 Listening and speaking

a Listen to an interview with a movie critic and note the reasons why Hollywood is still an important center for the movie industry.

b Listen to the interview again. Mark the sentences T (true) or F (false).

1 Hollywood movies which are distributed worldwide usually make money. T ○ F ○
2 Hollywood makes more movies than any other place in the world. T ○ F ○
3 It doesn't normally cost as much to make movies outside the U.S. T ○ F ○
4 Hollywood movies always make money. T ○ F ○
5 The movie *Titanic* wasn't filmed in the United States. T ○ F ○

c Some movie critics say all Hollywood movies follow the same old formula: happy start, terrible problem, hero or heroine and a happy ending. What do you think? Talk about the Hollywood movies you have seen.

3 Speaking and reading

a In pairs, discuss these questions. Then read the article quickly to check your answers.

1 Which country has the biggest movie industry in the world?
2 What are the characteristics of the movies produced there?

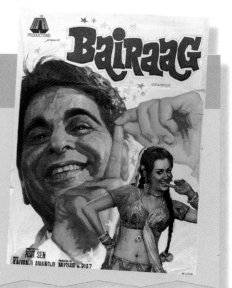

BOLLYWOOD

Everyone has heard of Tom Cruise, Leonardo DiCaprio, Julia Roberts and Cameron Díaz, but what about Aishwarya Rai, Dilip Kumar and Sunil Dutt? These names may not mean much to you, but for millions of movie-goers they are household names: they are stars of Indian movies. Many of these movies are made in Bombay, now often known as "Bollywood". India produces 900 full-length feature films a year, compared with Hollywood's 300. These movies are not only seen by India's huge population of one billion people but by Indian communities in many other parts of the world.
In Britain alone there are two million Asian British.
Most of them are fans of Bollywood movies.

Indian movies are very different from the typical Hollywood blockbuster. They offer romance (but no sex), stylized violence, dance and music. No one seeing a Bollywood movie wants to feel depressed so there is always a happy ending, where boy gets girl and the hero triumphs over hardened criminals. And no Bollywood movie is a blockbuster unless it is seen by at least 100 million people!

The latest development of the Indian movie business is a new 24-hour satellite channel: B4U (Bollywood for You). This channel will broadcast Indian programs to millions of fans at home as well as in other countries where there is an audience. It will also give them a wide variety of entertainment, documentary and news programs. It really will contain something for everybody!

b Read the article again and answer the questions.

1 How did the name "Bollywood" develop?
2 Why is the Indian movie industry so important?
3 Where is the market for Indian movies?
4 What does a blockbuster mean in India?
5 What is B4U and how does it work?

4 Grammar builder: indefinite pronouns

a Look at these examples of indefinite pronouns. How could you rephrase the words in bold? How do you express the same ideas in your own language?

1 ***Everyone*** *has heard of Tom Cruise, Leonardo DiCaprio, Julia Roberts and Cameron Díaz.*
2 ***No one*** *seeing a Bollywood movie wants to feel depressed.*
3 *It really will contain **something** for **everybody**!*

b Complete the chart with indefinite pronouns.

	People	Things	Places
every-	everyone, everybody		everywhere
some-		something	
any-			anywhere
no-	no one		

c Complete the sentences with the correct indefinite pronoun.

1 Has .... seen my cup?
2 I rang the door bell but .... answered.
3 .... is wrong with this computer. The monitor is blank.
4 These days cell phones are ....
5 It's raining so hard I can't see ....
6 The movie was good but there was hardly .... there.

d Read the statements, then check with your classmates to see if these are true or not for them.

1 Nobody has seen a Bollywood movie.
2 Nobody loves horror movies.
3 Everybody likes comedy movies.
4 Somebody goes to the movies every week.

Language assistant

Indefinite pronouns are singular and take singular verbs. However, in everyday speech we often use *they / their* when we do not know the sex of the person involved in the action.

*Everyone feels nervous when **they** take an exam.*

*Look. Someone left **their** wallet on the chair.*

LANGUAGE for life:

franchises

① Talking about franchises

You are thinking about moving into the franchise business. It is one of the fastest growing market areas in the world, and that means you have to be the best to make it!

What do you know about franchises? Check out your knowledge by reading the definitions below.

A **franchise** is an authority that is given by a company to someone, allowing them to sell its goods or services.

In most cases, a **franchisee** needs to pay a **franchise fee** to use the name of the product or service, plus further sums for the initial inventory as well as furniture, equipment and store construction.

The **company** continues to get a royalty percentage on gross sales and a percentage for promotion. In return, in many cases the company will help select and design the store, plan and order the initial merchandise and provide training for staff.

Franchises are common in several major industries, such as fast food, candy, cosmetics, sportswear and coffee stores.

② Choosing a franchise

OK. You've decided to go into the franchise business. You have to come up with a business plan to raise money. Look at the list below and label each item 1, 2 or 3 according to these aspects of starting a franchise.

1 = calculating costs involved in opening a franchise
2 = analyzing the potential demand for the product
3 = deciding where to put your franchise

- *Size of market* ◯
- *Amount of investment needed* ◯
- *Market growth* ◯
- *Locations for your store* ◯
- *Profitability of product or service* ◯
- *Image of product or service* ◯
- *Age of customers* ◯
- *Competition in the area* ◯

③ Case study: Candy Express

Candy Express is a good example of a franchise. In this case the product is confectionery. Imagine you are thinking about buying a franchise from Candy Express.

Look through this information on the company and underline anything that will help you make your decision.

The sale of candy and other confectionery products in the U.S. is worth $12 billion a year and is growing fast. With dual-income families producing more disposable income and with increasingly hectic lifestyles, sales of convenient ready-to-eat foods are at an all-time high. The primary market locations for Candy Express stores are shopping malls, but airports and transportation terminals, high-profile shopping streets and amusement parks are also popular locations.

Candy Express uses creative store designs and colorful presentation of quality chocolate, candy and gift products. Candies are sold at a single per pound price in a self-serve "pick-n-mix" format.

The company has been in the U.S. market for 14 years and has franchise agreements with many countries worldwide. It has 40 U.S. franchises. Average

sales rose 8.5% last year. It provides franchisees with a range of services, which include assistance with site selection, store design and construction, delivery of fixtures and products, on-site training from its 550-page operations manual, store merchandising and grand opening. There is continuous support to maintain a high level of sales, both in advertising and the development of new products.

A franchisee typically needs between $175,000 and $195,000 to start, which includes a $35,000 franchise fee, $25,000 for the initial inventory and the rest for furniture, fixtures and store construction.

④ Opening

⑤ Raising the money

You're convinced! Now, where would be the best place to locate your candy franchise store and what ideas could you use for a grand opening and eye-catching promotion?

Use the points in 2 and 3 to help you produce a short plan for your store.

The big day has come. Your plan is ready and you are going to present it to your bank. If it's good, they'll lend you the money and a dream will become reality. Good luck with the presentation!

Unit 4 Family, friends and colleagues

1 Brothers and sisters

1 Speaking and reading

a What do you know about these pop stars? Look at the title of the article and discuss what you understand by it.

b Read the article quickly. Is the description of brotherly love similar to your ideas?

Brotherly love

Brothers Noel and Liam Gallagher are famous for being members of the rock band *Oasis* – Noel is the songwriter and lead guitarist and Liam is the lead singer – but also for their fights and arguments. Since the group was founded in Manchester, England, in 1991, the brothers' notoriously volatile relationship has constantly been in the public eye. Incredible arguments have cut short several tours and in one case Liam abandoned a tour of the U.S. 15 minutes before the plane was due to take off.

The Gallaghers come from a working-class family of five brothers in Manchester. Their mother worked in a school and their father walked out on the family.

As boys, the brothers were respectable, responsible people rather than rebels. Liam formed the band with some friends and Noel joined later. Although the band started off by charging only $28.00 each to play at a concert, both Gallagher brothers are now millionaires. But they can't get along with each other and the band has been on the verge of breaking up several times because of differences between them.

In spite of all the problems, their first album in two years, *Standing on the Shoulder of Giants*, sold 100,000 copies on the first day of its release in 2000. Ironically, the album was the first on the band's own label, Big Brother. For the moment, Oasis and the Gallaghers live on.

c Work in pairs, A and B. Read the article again. A fill in 1 to 4 in the chart and B fill in 5 to 8. Then ask questions to complete your chart.

Oasis fact chart	
1 Date group was founded	
2 First names of Gallagher brothers	
3 Brothers' roles in group	
4 Hometown of Gallagher family	
5 Mother's workplace	
6 Name of a recent album	
7 Copies sold on first day of release	
8 Name of band's record label	

2 Word builder: suffixes

a The adjectives *respectable* and *responsible* come from the verbs *respect* and *respond*: the suffixes *-able* and *-ible* make them into adjectives. Use one of these suffixes to make adjectives from the list of words: *-able, -ate, -ful, -ible*.

> like   agree   care   sense   consider   thought   depend
> rely   affection   social   knowledge   play

b Work in groups of three. Say which of the adjectives apply to you and which definitely don't.

3 Speaking and listening

a Discuss these questions in pairs.

1 Are you an only child or do you have any brothers or sisters?
2 If you are one of several children, are you the oldest, middle or youngest child?
3 Do you think your character has anything to do with being the oldest, middle or youngest child in your family?

b Listen to the first part of an interview with a family expert and note why Dr. Wong thinks birth order is so important.

c Listen to the interview again and write the missing adjectives in the mind maps.

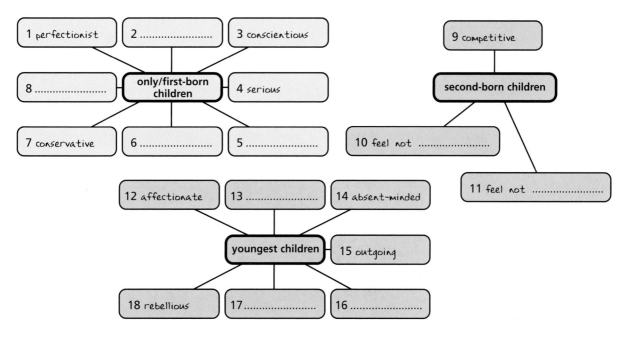

1 perfectionist	2	3 conscientious
8	only/first-born children	4 serious
7 conservative	6	5 ....

| 9 competitive |
| second-born children |
| 10 feel not .... |
| 11 feel not .... |

12 affectionate	13	14 absent-minded
youngest children	15 outgoing
18 rebellious	17	16 ....

d In groups, look back at exercise 3a. Have you changed your ideas after listening to the interview? What other factors do you think can influence children's characters? Make a list and compare your ideas with your group.

2 All you need is love

1 Speaking

In groups, talk about the picture and identify the event. How do you celebrate this event?

2 Listening and speaking

a Listen to the conversation between Vicky and Sam and match the opinion with the correct person.

1	Vicky is	a)	cynical about Valentine's Day.
2	Sam is	b)	in favor of the idea of Valentine's Day.

b Listen to the conversation again and note the arguments for and against Valentine's Day.

c What do you think about Valentine's Day? Discuss your ideas in groups.

3 Grammar builder: review of present tenses

a Complete the conversation with the present simple or present progressive tense.

Alan: Hi, Jean. How's it going?

Jean: Alan. Long time no see. What (1) .... (do) these days?

Alan: I (2) .... (work) in advertising now. And you?

Jean: I still (3) .... (write) short stories. I've had quite a lot published.

Alan: Good for you. Where (4) .... you .... (live) now?

Jean: In the same apartment. I (5) .... (try) to buy a house but prices (6) .... (get) so high. Are you still a soccer fanatic?

Alan: Er, I guess so. I (7) .... (go) to the game every Saturday. Trouble is, the soccer stadium (8) .... (be) really cold this time of the year. Five below zero last weekend!

Jean: Look. I (9) .... (meet) a friend for coffee in ten minutes. Would you like to join us?

Alan: Oh, I (10) .... (wait) for my girlfriend. Can she come too?

Jean: Sure.

b **1 Which examples of the present simple from the conversation correspond to the following uses? Write the numbers.**

a) Habits and routines: .... b) Permanent situations: ....

c) Facts: ....

2 Which examples of the present progressive correspond to the following?

d) Actions happening now or around now: ....

e) Temporary actions or situations: ....

f) Changes and developments: ....

g) A planned future event: ....

3 In which examples can you use either the present simple or present progressive? ....

4 Reading and speaking

a Read the article and choose the most suitable heading for each paragraph.

1 Communication 2 Beliefs about roles, relationships, marriage and family

3 Interests 4 Decision-making

b What factors are important for happiness and success in a relationship?

According to research, similarity increases happiness in almost all important areas of a relationship. These areas are:

a) .... These include beliefs about sex roles, togetherness versus privacy, philosophy of life and religious beliefs, beliefs about financial affairs as well as social issues, including politics.

b) .... In general, the most important issue in a relationship is that both partners feel that the decisions being made are in their best interests and lead to their overall happiness (win-win outcomes). A situation where both people feel they get their way in conflicts about half the time contributes to **both** persons' happiness.

c) .... Research shows that similar communication beliefs and styles tend to cause people to be happier together. Some people are better communicators and listeners than others. Honest, open, positive expression of feelings and thoughts on a regular basis creates an intimacy that is very important.

d) .... Especially those directly related to the relationship. The more similar the interest, generally the happier people are. These may be recreation interests, physical attractiveness, career interests and achievements, skills and abilities, other resources, e.g. money, material possessions, friends.

c Read the article again and answer the questions.

1 Why could different political views be a problem in a relationship?

2 What do you understand by win-win outcomes?

3 How might a partner feel if they always lose arguments?

4 What's the best way of creating intimacy in a relationship?

5 What type of material interests might exist in a relationship?

d In groups, talk about relationships you know and say why you think they are successful or unsuccessful.

3 Working relations

1 Word builder: words for gesture, posture and voice

a Put the words in the appropriate column
(or columns) in the table. Do the words convey
a positive, negative or neutral meaning?

frown wave shout point laugh slouch smile
stare nod yawn lean glare shake whisper

Body	Voice	Face	Hands	Head

b Choose the most suitable word in each sentence.

1 The committee *nodded / shook* their heads in agreement.

2 Jerry was so surprised he just *glared / stared* at me.

3 Margaret is *leaning / slouching* in her chair. I think she's bored.

4 The team members didn't understand the proposal. Several of them were *yawning / frowning*.

5 During the manager's speech, Pamela *shouted / whispered* to me that she was hungry.

2 Speaking, writing and listening

a In groups, discuss what kinds of factors interfere with effective communication
at work, e.g. how you feel about the person who is speaking to you, or the
means of communication – phone, face to face. Write down your ideas.

b Listen to a training session on communication. Number these points in the
order that they are mentioned. Check your list with a classmate.

a) Different perceptions of a problem or topic ◯

b) Use or absence of non-verbal communication ◯

c) Distrust of the person giving the message ◯

d) Emotional reactions ◯

e) Language differences ◯

f) Specialized terms ◯

c Listen to the session again and answer the questions.

1 Why can people interpret the same information in different ways?

2 Why can language be a problem in effective communication?

3 Which solutions are suggested for the problems of noise?

4 How can emotional reactions affect communication?

5 Which four non-verbal types of communication are mentioned
by the speaker?

6 What is distrust directly linked to?

3 Grammar builder: verbs which do not take the progressive

a Look at the sentences and say which are correct and which are incorrect uses of the present progressive.

1 I'm really liking classical music.
2 You're not listening to me!
3 We're not knowing the answer to this question.
4 This fish is tasting salty.
5 Jane's hoping to change jobs.

b Complete the sentences with the correct form of the verb (present simple or progressive).

1 Alex .... (stay) with his granny for a few days.
2 Tania .... (want) to go to the movies tonight.
3 They .... (not / understand) how the accident happened.
4 I .... (see) what you mean.
5 This meat .... (smell) strange.
6 Ssh! We .... (listen) to a really good CD.

> ### Language assistant
> Many verbs are not usually used in the progressive: verbs that refer to a state which is not normally a continuing process (e.g. *see, hear, like, want, believe, know*), and verbs which refer to an action that is instantaneous (e.g. *smell, taste, shut, throw, smash*). Verbs taking the progressive usually have a human subject actively controlling the action (or state) expressed by the verb e.g. *Mike's looking at that car.*

4 Reading and speaking

a Take the quiz and then check your answers.

HOW GOOD A COMMUNICATOR ARE YOU?

1 When you are having a conversation with someone, do you
a) pay close attention to every word?
b) get a bit distracted after a while?
c) let your mind wander and say "Hmmm, yes, right!"?

2 While someone is speaking to you do you normally
a) let them speak and encourage them to continue?
b) sometimes interrupt to clarify points?
c) constantly interrupt whenever you disagree or want to say something?

3 While you listen to someone do you
a) keep an open mind as everyone is entitled to their opinion?
b) make some judgements about what they are saying?
c) immediately decide if they are talking nonsense?

4 During a conversation do you
a) maintain eye contact with the speaker or listener?
b) occasionally look at other things?
c) make sure you look at anything interesting that's happening around you?

5 When you talk to someone do you normally
a) say what you honestly think?
b) sometimes change your views if you think someone won't like them?
c) say whatever you think the other person wants to hear?

Scores
Mostly As You are a highly effective communicator and a good listener.
Mostly Bs You communicate well but there's room for improvement.
Mostly Cs Communication isn't your strong point. Take a course in communication as soon as possible!

b Is there really a difference in the way we communicate at work and with our friends and family? If so, what are the differences and how do you account for them?

LANGUAGE for life:

foreign *exchanges*

① Making contact

You have the chance to participate in an exchange program for one year with a foreign student. You will live and study for a year in his / her country and he / she will come to your country.

Complete the fourth profile below for yourself. Then look at the three exchange possibilities and decide which one you have the most in common with.

Name:	Nadine Lecroix
Age:	20
Nationality:	French
Hometown:	Lille
Family:	1 brother (14)
Main activity:	2nd year economics student, Lille University
Languages:	French, English
Interests:	Travel, swimming, food
Profile:	Outgoing, enthusiastic, works and plays hard
Other info:	Aquarius

Name:	Charlotte Austen
Age:	20
Nationality:	Canadian
Hometown:	Vancouver
Family:	1 sister
Main activity:	Hotel Management course – Vancouver Community College
Languages:	English, French, Spanish
Interests:	Cooking, sightseeing, cycling
Profile:	Sociable, good sense of humor, great dancer!
Other info:	Interested in Latin America

Name:	Chris Martinez
Age:	19
Nationality:	Australian
Hometown:	Melbourne
Family:	2 sisters, 1 brother
Main activity:	1st year media studies student
Languages:	Spanish, English
Interests:	Photography, reading, music – playing the guitar
Profile:	Quiet, serious but friendly and sings well
Other info:	Writing first novel

Name:	....
Age:	....
Nationality:	....
Hometown:	....
Family:	....
Main activity:	....
Languages:	....
Interests:	....
Profile:	....
Other info:	....

Arrangements

So you're going on a foreign exchange for a year. Congratulations! Now you'll have to make plans.

Write the first ten things on your list.

Important things
for the exchange

1	2
3	4
5	6
7	8
9	10

OK, let's look at that list. Did you include a present for the host family you're going to stay with?

Listen to Carol talking about what she had to organize for her exchange in Ecuador. How close is your list? Make a note of any useful advice she gives.

Adapting to another culture

Adapting to another culture is not always as easy as you first think. The big challenge is to learn the language of the country. If you speak the language, many aspects of the culture are more accessible. There may be other big differences, such as the type of food and when people have their meals. In some countries the main meal of the day is at midday, in others it is in the evening. Food may be spicier or heavier than you are used to, with dishes and elements which are completely new. Other factors can also vary from one country to another. Time may be more or less flexible. For instance, Anglo-Saxon cultures tend to be more inflexible about time than some other cultures. Stores may close and open at different times and holidays can differ completely from one country to another.

What would you miss most about your country if you went abroad for some time? What aspects of your culture would be most difficult for an English-speaking foreigner to adapt to?

Write to the exchange student you selected from the profiles. Include a short paragraph introducing yourself and attach your profile. Also, ask him / her questions about things you think you should know before you arrive in their country.

Hosting

It's your turn to host a student for six months. Now you have to make some plans. Your guest will go to your college and take language classes as well.

Think about the following areas and note some ideas for each category.

- People to meet – at college, family, friends
- Important places in your town – stores, library, markets, post office, banks
- Health – doctor, dentist
- Sports – places to work out

- Having fun – movie theaters, clubs, coffee shops, restaurants
- Places of interest – museums, historical sites, art galleries
- Places to visit in other parts of your country or region

Discuss your ideas with another student.

2 Learning check

1 Progress check

a Complete the sentences with the pairs of nouns in the box. Use the correct form, i.e. noun + noun or noun + 's + noun.

> boy / foot   philosophy / class   husband / coat   cat / ears   wine / glass

1 Would you like something to drink? Pass me that .... and I'll fill it for you.
2 Marilyn left the room, fetched her .... and insisted that they leave the party immediately.
3 I love the soft, velvety feel of the fur on ....
4 I've just enrolled in a .... at the local college. It sounds really interesting.
5 The train door slammed shut, trapping the .... as he struggled to move away.

b Choose the best completion (a–c) for each sentence.

6 This is impossible! I don't think .... can do it.
   a) anybody   **b)** no one   **c)** none
7 Hey! What ....? Leave my car alone!
   a) do you do   **b)** you do   **c)** are you doing
8 It was an extremely difficult exam, and .... passed it.
   a) anyone   **b)** nobody   **c)** somebody
9 Hi! I'm glad you could come. .... the party?
   a) Are you liking   **b)** Do you enjoy   **c)** Are you enjoying
10 .... is as difficult as being a really good parent.
    a) Anything   **b)** No one   **c)** Nothing

c Read the sentences below. Check (✔) the correct sentences and correct the errors you find.

Everyone ~~were~~ very happy at the end of the film   ..was..................

11 We couldn't find the keys nowhere.   ....
12 I'm staying here until Sam arrives.   ....
13 We saw no one we knew at the party.   ....
14 They are wanting to move to a bigger house.   ....
15 I don't enjoy the concert. I'm leaving.   ....

2 Proficiency check

a Read the information about scholarships. Then look at the statements and mark them T (true) or F (false).

SCHOLARSHIPS IN SOCIAL SCIENCES

The ABCI Foundation is offering twenty postgraduate scholarships in social and educational areas at certain American, British, Canadian and Irish universities. These scholarships are only for people who are not citizens of any of those countries. They will run from the start of the next academic year and applications are invited immediately.

Candidates must have at least two years' work experience in their area since graduation and be working currently in their own country. They should be able to take one or two years off with the right to return to their current position or a higher position with the same employer.

Applicants should send a CV, copies of professional qualifications and a letter from their current employer agreeing to the terms to Monica Schultz at the address below.

---

1 The scholarships are for college graduates only.
T◯   F◯

2 Successful candidates can study wherever they like.
T◯   F◯

3 The scholarships are not for American citizens.
T◯   F◯

4 Candidates can apply from the beginning of next year.
T◯   F◯

5 People who have just graduated are not eligible.
T◯   F◯

6 To be eligible, candidates must not be working abroad.
T◯   F◯

7 Candidates must be able to return to their present position.
T◯   F◯

8 Applications should be sent to the address at the top.
T◯   F◯

b Read the letter and choose the best completion (a–d) for each sentence.

February 7

Dear Mr. Aguilera,

We are pleased to inform you that you have been selected for interview for an ABCI Scholarship. This is not an offer of a scholarship, but still part of the selection process.

If you still wish to pursue this opportunity, please call me between the hours of 8.30 a.m. and 5.30 p.m. on any weekday this month for an appointment. The interviews will be held at our offices in the last week of next month. Since your only TOEFL score was achieved several years ago, it is no longer valid. You will be required to supply a new score at the interview. Please make arrangements in this respect.

Yours sincerely,

Monica Schultz

1 Mr. Aguilera is being offered:
   a) a scholarship examination.
   b) a TOEFL interview.
   c) a scholarship interview.
   d) a scholarship.

2 Mr. Aguilera can call for an appointment:
   a) this week.
   b) for a month.
   c) in the next three weeks.
   d) in three weeks' time.

3 The interviews will be:
   a) at the end of February.
   b) at the end of March.
   c) after next month.
   d) at the end of the month.

4 Mr. Aguilera:
   a) has taken TOEFL but failed.
   b) has never taken TOEFL.
   c) took TOEFL several times in the past.
   d) has to take TOEFL again.

Unit 5 The best of the past

1 The history of pop culture

1 Speaking

Look at the picture of Elvis Presley, an idol in the 1950s and 60s. Then discuss these questions.

1 John Lennon of The Beatles once said: "Before Elvis, there was nothing." What do you think he meant?
2 Why do you think teenagers loved Elvis and many parents were upset by him?
3 Do you know anything about Elvis? Who do you think is a modern-day equivalent of Elvis?

2 Reading and speaking

a Sentences 1–6 are paraphrases of central ideas in the article below. Some of the paraphrases contain factual errors. Read the article and correct the errors.

1 In the U.S., as in many other countries, there is a strong pop culture, dominated by young people.
2 Great differences in clothing, music and so on have always existed between young people and older people in the U.S.
3 The generation gap began during World War II.
4 One of the main elements of the generation gap is rock music.
5 In the sixties, music changed to reflect the growing social consciousness of young people.
6 In the U.S., the differences between generations became less marked after the sixties.

THEIR OWN CULTURE

When we think of pop culture, we usually think of the very latest styles of music, entertainment and fashion. We also think of young people because pop culture is really youth culture; young people are the ones most interested in the "latest thing". Parents are often horrified by the music, clothing and hairstyles of their children! But in the U.S., at least, it hasn't always been that way. Though parents and children have surely always had their differences, until the mid-1950s styles of dress and entertainment weren't really very different between older people and young people.

After World War II, the U.S. became a very prosperous country. Young people had more and more spending money and many had their own cars, which gave them a new sense of independence. Around 1955 a revolutionary change took place which would create a vast difference between generations – rock and roll arrived on the scene, with Elvis Presley as its undisputed king. Presley sang of love, personal freedom and identity crises, all of vital interest to young people. And he danced in a wild, free style that delighted teenagers and upset parents. The generation gap was born.

The new youth culture continued to grow in the 1960s. Music became "heavier" and more political, with many songs protesting against war and social injustice. Most young people wore clothing which was radically different from that of their parents – very old jeans, exaggerated bell bottoms, mini skirts and wild patterns and colors. Movies, TV programs and advertising began to be directed specifically at young people. They were called the Now Generation.

It is said that you can never go back, and certainly the youth culture which began in the 50s and 60s has not disappeared. Pop music and clothing styles have changed, but young people's tastes today are as different from the tastes of their parents as *theirs* were different from *their* parents' tastes. And the beat goes on ...

b Discuss styles and preferences of teenagers / young adults and their parents in your country.

1 Do young people wear different clothes and listen to different music from their parents?

2 Do older and younger generations tend to do social activities together or separately?

3 Do you think there is a bigger generation gap between young people and older people today than there was between your parents and their parents? Why or why not?

3 Listening and writing

a Listen to a radio program about U.S. youth culture. Do the two sociologists have the same opinions about it?

b Listen again. Take notes of the positive and negative aspects mentioned by the sociologists.

4 Speaking and writing

a In exercise 2b, you talked about whether there is a youth culture or a generation gap in your country. In groups, now discuss these questions.

1 How does a generation gap normally manifest itself? One way, for example, might be in arguments between parents and their children over what clothing is appropriate for certain situations.

2 Do you think young people need to have their own culture? Why or why not?

3 What personal experiences have you had of the generation gap?

b Share your ideas with the class.

c What advice would you give to someone from an older generation who wants to get along better with young people? In pairs, make a list of points, then write a paragraph explaining your advice.

You're not going out like THAT, are you?

2 Revolutionaries past and present

1 Reading and listening

a Read and listen to this excerpt from a poem by Longfellow, a famous American poet. It is about Paul Revere. Who was he? Why did he become a legend of the American Revolution?

Paul Revere's Ride
by Henry Wadsworth Longfellow

Listen my children and you shall hear
Of the midnight ride of Paul Revere.
On the eighteenth of April, in seventy-five,
Hardly a man is now alive
Who remembers that famous day and year.
He said to his friend, "If the British march
By land or sea from the town tonight,
Hang a lantern aloft in the belfry arch
Of the North Church tower as a signal light,
One if by land and two if by sea;
And I on the opposite shore will be,
Ready to ride and spread the alarm
Through every Middlesex village and farm,
For the country folk to be up and to arm."

b Read the text and check your answers to exercise 1a.

It was a dark night in Boston on April 18, 1775, and (1) there was tension and fear in the air. (2) The American colonies were fighting the British for their independence, and there was a rumor that the British were going to attack that night. Paul Revere – artist, silversmith and revolutionary – was waiting for information about whether the British would attack by land or by sea so that he could warn revolutionary leaders. Suddenly, there were two lanterns glowing from the church tower, a sign that the enemy would arrive by water, across the Charles River. (3) Revere leaped on his horse and galloped through the countryside at full speed, slowing at each house along the way to shout "The British are coming!" Revere was arrested by British soldiers, but (4) not before he had warned the leaders and prevented a surprise attack on American troops in Boston. Boston was the center of the American Revolution, and if Paul Revere hadn't made his courageous ride, (5) the outcome of the revolution might have been very different.

For people who live in America, history is full of stories of heroic freedom fighters like George Washington, Miguel Hidalgo, Simón Bolívar and José Martí. We tend to think of revolutionary heroes as people who fought to free their countries from oppressive governments in the 18th and 19th centuries, but in more recent history there have been people who fought for other causes. Martin Luther King Jr. became a martyr in the fight for racial equality in the United States in the 1950s and 60s. Rigoberta Menchú has spent years of her life supporting the rights of indigenous people in Central America. Other people have fought for causes like peace, the rights of animals and environmental protection. We think of heroes as people who risk their lives, but they may also be people who risk their jobs or who put good causes before personal gain or comfort. These people may fight smaller, quieter revolutions, but they are revolutions all the same.

c Find sentences or phrases in the text that support these statements, i.e. that prove to you these statements are correct.

1 It wasn't certain that the British were going to attack that night.

2 Revere helped the American soldiers.

3 People associate revolutionaries with the past.

4 Revolutionaries don't always fight for freedom of a country.

2 Grammar builder: the past

Look at some of the ways we use tenses to describe the past. Then look at the phrases in blue in the text opposite. Match each phrase (numbered) with one of the functions below.

1 .... 2 .... 3 .... 4 .... 5 ....

1 To describe a setting, we often use
   a) the past simple: *The night **was** dark and the town slept peacefully.*
   b) the past continuous: *An old man **was watching** the moon rise from his window.*
   c) *there was / were:* ***There were** thousands of stars and **there wasn't** a cloud.*

2 To describe actions or events, we often use
   a) the past simple: *A dog **started** to bark.*
   b) the past perfect: *The man **had checked** the locks before he went to bed.*
   c) the past continuous: *He **was getting** into bed when he heard a noise.*

3 To make deductions about a person or situation in the past, we often use
   a) *must have: He **must have** been frightened.*
   b) *may / might have: The noise **may have** been an animal.*
   c) *couldn't have: It **couldn't have** been an animal because it was inside the house.*

3 Speaking

In groups, talk about revolutionaries in your country.

1 Are there historical heroes like José Martí or Paul Revere? Why are they considered heroes?

2 Are there any modern revolutionaries? What causes do (or did) they support? Are (or were) they considered heroes or troublemakers by most people?

3 In your opinion, are (or were) their causes legitimate? Why or why not?

4 Writing

a **In pairs or groups, write a story about a heroic act. It can be a real event from history or you can invent a story. Your story should include:**

- background or setting: *It was the year ... / He was feeling ... / There were ...*
- the event: *He ran ... / Everyone had gone ... / Everyone was shouting ...*
- an opinion or speculation: *It must have been ... / They couldn't have wanted to ...*

b **Read your story to your class. Vote on the best story.**

3 Viewpoint

1 Listening and reading

a You are going to listen to a lecture. Look at the photographs. What do you think the lecture is about?

b Listen to the lecture and check your answer. Does the lecturer think life was probably better or worse in the past than it is today?

c Listen again and complete the first column of the table.

	Lecturer	E-mail
Traffic	terrible – lots of carriages, etc.	
Cleanliness		
Pollution		little – no autos, so no carbon monoxide
Health		

d Now read the e-mail and complete the second column of the table. Does the writer have any of the same points of view as the lecturer?

Hello, Frank. I thought I'd write you an e-mail as I'm sitting in a taxi, stuck in London rush hour traffic. You know, even though I love conveniences like e-mail, sometimes I wish I had lived here in the 19th century, not the 21st! Just imagine London with no automobiles and no traffic jams – heaven! I would have been perfectly happy to travel in one of those elegant Victorian carriages. I think the city must have been much cleaner, too. Today's automobile emissions make all the buildings dirty. And they fill the air with carbon monoxide, of course. On some days the air is really terrible, and I wish for the cleaner atmosphere of an earlier century. I imagine that a century ago you could look up and see blue sky every day. Yes, it would have been nice to live in quieter, cleaner Victorian London, but on the other hand I wouldn't want to give up things like modern medicine either! There were all those diseases like typhoid, cholera and tuberculosis and no antibiotics to cure them.

Well, enough speculation about life in Victorian England! Our meetings are all arranged for next week and I'll be in New York on Monday. I'm looking forward to seeing you and to working out the final details of the project.

See you soon,
Fiona

2 Word builder: recording vocabulary

a **Different people have different ways of recording vocabulary. Organize these words from the lecture and the e-mail by each of the three different techniques.**

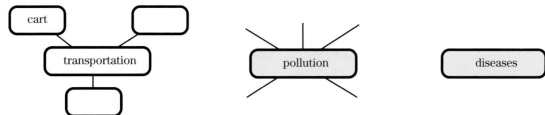

cholera cart diphtheria waste emissions carriage smoke tuberculosis sewage wagon carbon monoxide typhoid

1 Mind maps

Some people like to make mind maps of words with related meanings. This visual technique can help you remember sets of words related to specific categories. Complete the mind maps with the words from the box.

cart — transportation

pollution

diseases

2 Contexts

Other people like to think of vocabulary in sentences or groups of words which go together. The context helps them to remember the words. Complete these phrases with words from the box, and write phrases for the others.

The river was polluted with ....
.... from automobiles
a horse-drawn ....
People died from ....

3 Translations

Other people like to make lists of words with translations in their own language. Write translations of the words which are not cognates (similar in your language).

b **Thinking about these three techniques, which did you like? Which didn't you like? Which have you never tried?**

Learning tip

Try different ways of organizing and studying vocabulary to find the way which works best for you.

3 Writing and speaking

a **In pairs, imagine you are historians living 100 years from now. You have been asked to write an article about your city at the beginning of the 21st century. One of you has a very negative opinion of what life must have been like and the other has a very positive opinion. Write the article from your point of view. Look back at the table in exercise 1c for ideas.**

b **Work with another pair. Read and discuss your articles.**

1 Do the two positive articles say similar things? What about the two negative articles?

2 How do you think historians a hundred years from now will view your city at the turn of the century? What things will they think were positive? What things will they think were negative?

LANGUAGE for life:

project *management*

1 Model cases

UNESCO (United Nations Educational, Scientific and Cultural Organization) is an international organization concerned with the preservation of heritage sites around the world. The places on the UNESCO heritage list range from endangered wilderness areas and historical sites to outstanding modern architecture.

Imagine that you are on a committee appointed by your government to identify potential UNESCO sites in your country. First, look at these examples of UNESCO sites and answer the questions.

- *Are there any similar sites in your country?*
- *Do you know whether they are included on the UNESCO list?*

If you would like to check for UNESCO sites in your country, you can search the Internet under the UNESCO heritage list.

Tikal National Park, Guatemala

Reasons for inscription: One of the major sites of the Mayan civilization from the 6th century BC to the 10th century AD. Site contains outstanding examples of Mayan architecture, including temples, palaces and public squares.

Río Plátano Biosphere Reserve, Honduras

Reasons for inscription: One of few remaining rainforests in Central America. A wide variety of animal and plant life. Over 2,000 indigenous people still live in the forest.

Problems: Destruction of forest by timber industry. Uncontrolled hunting of animals. Needs better park management. Potential hydroelectric project may have negative effects.

University City, Caracas, Venezuela

Reasons for inscription: Excellent example of Modern Movement in architecture, by Venezuelan architect Carlos Raúl Villanueva and other distinguished artists. University City demonstrates how architecture and art can combine function and beauty, in a style appropriate to tropical climate.

② Choosing a site

With your committee, follow the procedures listed below.

1 Make a list of potential sites in your country and categorize them as E (ecological), H (historical) or C (cultural). Include the sites you discussed in 1 and add others if possible.

2 You've been told that only one site from your country will be included in the list this year. Choose the site you prefer and write reasons why you feel it should be chosen.

3 Discuss your reasons with your committee. The committee must come to an agreement on one site.

4 After you have agreed on the site, review your reasons for inclusion on the UNESCO list and add further reasons if possible.

5 Look back at the description of the Río Plátano Reserve. Consider any existing or potential problems with your site. Is the ecology of the area threatened? Is the architecture in poor condition? Is uncontrolled tourism threatening the integrity of the site?

6 Complete the form below about your site.

7 As a class, discuss the heritage sites chosen by each group and decide which of the sites chosen would be the best candidate for the UNESCO list. Also, decide what could be done to solve any problems with the site.

PETITION FOR INCLUSION OF A SITE ON THE UNESCO WORLD HERITAGE LIST

Country: **Location:**
....

Type of site:
....

....

Description:
....

....

Reasons for inscription:
....

....

Existing or potential problems:
....

....

Unit 6 Our century

1 Future shock

1 Listening

In 1970, Alvin Toffler wrote a best-seller called *Future Shock* in which he predicted the effects that technology would have on our future. Listen to an excerpt from a college future studies class and answer these questions.

1 According to Alvin Toffler, what is future shock?
2 What effects did he think technology would have on people? Do you think he was correct?
3 What technological differences do the speakers mention between the 1970s and now?

2 Speaking and reading

a Discuss the following questions.

1 Do you know any science fiction books or movies? Which ones? What was your opinion of them?
2 Can you think of any science fiction that has predicted things that are part of our lives today?

b Read the introduction to the article and answer the questions.

1 According to the introduction, what purposes does science fiction serve?
2 Think of the science fiction you have seen or read. What was its main purpose?

THE WORLD OF SCIENCE FICTION

When many people think of science fiction, they think of silly late-night movies on TV, with giant, human-sized insects taking over the world or ugly green creatures invading from
5 some <u>remote</u> planet. This type of science fiction is intended simply to <u>provide</u> low-level entertainment. But there is also high-quality, interesting science fiction, which may have entertainment as one <u>aim</u>, but which can also
10 serve to predict the future or warn us about tendencies in our society.

c   **Now read the rest of the article and answer these questions.**

1   What is the main idea of the first paragraph?

2   In the second paragraph, why is Miles not happy in his new life?

An interesting question to consider is <u>whether</u> science fiction writers have occasionally been lucky in predicting inventions of the future or
15 whether they may have <u>actually</u> given scientists ideas for new inventions. For example, in 1870, Jules Verne wrote *20,000 Leagues Under the Sea*, in which men went to the bottom of the sea in a round metal container. The book preceded the
20 invention of the bathysphere by 64 years. Verne also predicted space travel, guided missiles, submarines, helicopters, air conditioning and the <u>motion picture</u>, long before any of those things were reality. By imagining such futuristic things,
25 could Jules Verne and other science fiction writers have been partly responsible for some of our technology today?

A very different type of science fiction is Woody Allen's 1973 comedy film *Sleeper*. In the
30 film, a health food store owner named Miles goes into the hospital for an operation and dies. His body is cryogenically frozen and forgotten for 200 years. In 2173, he is unfrozen and wakes up in the

35 world of the future. There is an oppressive government which demands complete
40 conformity from the people, but Miles joins a group of revolutionary activists who want to <u>overthrow</u> the
45 government. He escapes from the police by pretending to be an android and going to work as a kitchen robot, where he is surprised to find that things like red meat and cigarettes are now considered to be healthy. He is also <u>amazed</u> to see
50 enormous, genetically modified fruits and vegetables. Every convenience one could imagine exists in 2173, but Miles misses the less high-tech, intellectually freer world of 1973, when you could still get a good pastrami sandwich and a bad cup
55 of coffee in a New York diner.

3 Word builder: synonyms

a   **The words on the left below are underlined in the article. Match them with their synonyms. In each case, indicate how you arrived at the answer.**

1 = I already knew the word.   **2** = I figured it out from the context.

3 = It's similar to a word in my language.   **4** = I looked it up.

5 = Other (specify).

1   remote ....
2   provide ....
3   aim ....
4   whether ....
5   actually ....
6   motion picture ....
7   overthrow ....
8   amazed ....

a) very surprised
b) if
c) remove from power
d) distant
e) purpose
f) in fact
g) movie
h) give

Learning tip

Try to figure out a word from context before using your dictionary. You can try these strategies to find out the meaning of a word or phrase.
1 What does the context around the word or phrase tell you?
2 If the word or phrase is repeated, do new contexts give you more clues?
3 Is the word the same or similar to a word in your language?
4 Look at the grammar of the word, e.g. noun, verb, and look at prefixes or suffixes.

b   **Now look back at the article and work out the meaning of these words: *leagues* (line 17), *bathysphere* (line 20), *pastrami* (line 54). In groups, discuss your answers and, most importantly, how you got to them.**

2 The best intentions

1 Listening

On New Year's Eve, it is customary to make resolutions – promises to yourself or others about things you will do in the coming year. Listen to some people at a New Year's Eve party and write the resolutions that Steve, Sandra, Joe and Renée mention.

2 Speaking and reading

a Have you ever made any resolutions? Did you stick to them? Why or why not?

I was going to read more in English, but …

b Read this article about resolutions and take the test. What are some factors which are necessary for sticking to a resolution?

STICKING TO THOSE RESOLUTIONS!

How many people make New Year's Resolutions or other promises but fail to stick to them? Most resolutions don't survive more than a few weeks after people make them – if they even start them at all!

So what's the secret to sticking with plans and making them work? Here's a little test: read the three cases below. Which of the people do you think stuck to his or her New Year's resolution and why? Why do you think the others failed?

Martin: I'm going to lose thirty pounds by my birthday in March. I'm going to run three kilometers every day. If I go on an 800-calorie-a-day diet, I'll lose about three pounds a week. I will have lost the thirty pounds in ten weeks!

Susan: I'm going to save money so I can spend time in Spain when I graduate from college. I can work part-time two days a week and on Saturdays, so I can earn about $400 a month. My parents said that if I save $200 a month, they'll help me with the rest.

Mandy: I'm going to move to Hollywood and get a small part in a movie. I took some drama classes, so I have some acting experience. My boyfriend says I'm attractive enough to be an actress.

Did you guess correctly? The successful person was Susan. She made a realistic plan for saving money based on how much she could earn in her free time. She was also motivated by her parents' offer to help and she was content to reach her goal little by little.

Martin and Mandy, on the other hand, had unrealistic expectations of what they could do. Martin wanted to reduce his calorie intake to almost dangerous levels and he planned an overly ambitious exercise routine. Of course, he didn't stick to either one! Mandy should have done some research on the best ways to get into the difficult field of acting and she'd probably need several years of training first. These days, a pretty face and a few acting classes are not enough!

3 Grammar builder: future simple, *be going to* and future perfect

a Look at these examples from the listening in exercise 1 and answer the questions.

1 *I'm going to look for a new job.*
   When did Joe make the decision?
   a) at the moment of speaking ○   **b)** sometime in the past ○

2 *Uh, I'm not sure. I think I'll start going to the gym.*
   When did Sandra make the decision?
   a) at the moment of speaking ○   **b)** sometime in the past ○

3 What is the difference between *be going to* and *will* in this context?

b Look at this example of the future perfect and answer the questions.

I will have finished my Master's thesis by January.

1 Is the thesis finished now?
2 Will it be finished in January?

c Complete the conversation with *will* + verb, *be going to* + verb or future perfect.

Frank: (1) .... you still .... (live) in Spain, Susan?

Susan: Yes. By June I (2) .... (save) $4,000, so I (3) .... (try) to stay in Spain for six months to a year. What (4) .... you .... (do) after graduation?

Frank: I'm not sure. I (5) .... probably .... (take) a short vacation and then look for a summer job. I (6) .... (start) graduate school in the fall.

Susan: You (7) .... (be) in graduate school for a semester by the time I get back from Spain!

4 Pronunciation: showing interest

a Listen to three people talking to Renée. Can you hear any differences in the ways they speak?

b Listen again and match the speaker and the level of interest.

Speaker	Level of interest
1	**a)** very interested
2	**b)** interested
3	**c)** not interested

c Listen again and say the sentences. Try to copy the intonation.

5 Writing and speaking

a Write a resolution on a piece of paper. Explain how you plan to put your resolution into practice, and if possible, set a deadline for the results.

I'm going to lose weight. I'll stop eating candy and drinking soft drinks. I will have lost three kilos by next month.

b In groups, talk about each person's resolution. Is it realistic? Is there a good plan for carrying it out? Do you think the person will stick to the resolution?

3 Biosphere

1 Speaking and listening

a Look at the photograph before you listen to an interview.
In your opinion, what is Biosphere 2? What is its purpose?

b Now listen to the interview and answer these questions.

1 What is a biosphere?

2 What is the present purpose of Biosphere 2?

3 What was the purpose of the biosphere from 1991 to 1993?

4 What did the scientists say they had learned during that time?

2 Grammar builder: review of future forms

a In English, there are many ways to talk about the future, depending on how
the speaker sees the situation. Match the sentences with their meanings.

1 A party at Mary's house? No, it'll be boring.

2 The bus leaves in two hours.

3 I'm going to stay home and rest tonight.

4 By Friday, I will have written my paper.

5 I like this shirt. I think I'll buy it.

6 Watch out! You're going to fall!

7 I'm having dinner with my parents tonight.

8 This time next week, I'll be (living) in Boston.

9 If you don't study, you won't pass the test.

10 I'll call you tomorrow.

a) a promise

b) a plan or intention

c) an event which has been arranged

d) a prediction based on past experience

e) a decision which has just been made

f) a situation which will be true at a certain point in the future

g) a formally scheduled event

h) a possibility in the future

i) something that will be finished by a certain time in the future

j) a prediction based on present evidence

b Read the conversation and complete it with appropriate future forms.

A: Good luck with your exam.

B: Thanks. I (1) .... (finish) it by 4:00. I (2) ....(call) you then.

A: Sure. Hey, don't forget that the Johnsons (3) .... (come) for dinner tonight at 8:00.

B: Yeah, that (4) .... (be) fun. But is it OK if I get there about 9:30?

A: That's too late. We (5) .... (start) dinner before then. What about 9:00?

B: Uh, let's see. Yeah, there's a train at 8:30 which (6) .... (get) there at 8:50.

A: Fine. I (7) .... (see) you later.

B: Yeah. I (8) .... (enjoy) tonight after finishing this exam!

3 Reading and speaking

You have been asked to participate in a biosphere project. You have to choose
four people to live in a closed biosphere for a year. In groups, read the brief and
choose four of the people described. Give reasons for your choices.

They'll need a doctor when there are medical problems.

They're going to need a carpenter to help design and build houses.

Century 21 Biosphere

Aim: To see how well people can adjust to living in
a self-sufficient, closed environment, away from
family, friends and conveniences for one year.
Research may be important in relation to colonizing
space in the future.

Situation: One year in a biosphere of temperate
climate. Participants will produce their own food,
maintain and repair life support and telecommuni-
cations systems, build their own living quarters and
solve all problems related to biosphere operations as
well as interpersonal relationships.

Candidates

1 Female, 45, medical
doctor. Hobbies are
gardening and playing
chess. Recently divorced,
has 18-year-old son.

4 Female, 50, biochemist
specializing in nutrition
and food science. Hobby
is French cooking. Insulin-
dependent diabetic.

2 Male, 19, college student
in computer science.
Friends call him "Genius".
Lives with his family.
Hobby is computer games.

5 Male, 29, carpenter, no college
education. Currently working as
architect's apprentice. Hobby is
designing and building furniture.
Slightly claustrophobic.

3 Male, 52, botany professor.
Wife died last year and he
says he wants a change.
Hobbies are reading and
auto mechanics.

6 Female, 33, author, especially
interested in effects of
humorous literature in stress
management. Hobbies are
story-telling and carpentry.

4 Writing and speaking

a The project managers want to add a
fifth person to the biosphere team:
one person from your group. Write a
paragraph saying why you think you
would be a good addition to the
team already chosen by your group.

b Read your paragraph to your
committee. As a committee, decide
who is the strongest candidate for
the biosphere team.

*I believe that my skills and interests make me an
excellent candidate for the biosphere team. I'm
28 and have no health problems. I'm an ecologist
and I've worked on a project called Save the
Rainforests for three years. I enjoy working with
other people and I think I'm relaxed and outgoing.
My hobby is cooking. I'm married, but my wife is in
favor of my joining the biosphere team.*

LANGUAGE for life:
getting *involved*

① The problem

Let's imagine a town of about 50,000 people. We'll call it Greenwood and we'll put it in Mississippi. Greenwood is a pleasant town, but many of its residents are worried. About ten years ago, a software manufacturer and an automobile plant moved into the area. In the last ten years, many people have moved to Greenwood from large northern cities and the population has doubled. The ecosystem around Greenwood is beginning to be affected by the rapid growth.

A professor and a group of students at Greenwood Community College have formed a committee to think of ways to involve the community in improving Greenwood's environment. They are having a meeting to make a working list of the town's problems.

Listen to the meeting and complete the list.

Areas of concern

1 Care of public areas
* stray animals
* animal waste
* ....

2 Disposal of garbage
* no ....

3 Appearance of town
* ....
* more buildings and ....

Solutions

Getting involved

Listen to the second committee meeting. In what ways is the committee going to organize its efforts?

1 Ask **local businesses to donate money and supplies.**

2 Have neighborhood meetings to encourage ....

3 Ask.. ....

4 Get.. ....

The committee has made an outline of possible solutions to the problems listed in the first meeting.

Match the solutions below with the problems.

Problems

Care of public areas
1 Stray animals (f) ○
2 Animal waste ○
3 Littering ○ ○

Disposal of garbage
4 No recycling programs ○ ○

Appearance of town
5 Too many buildings, not enough plants ○
6 Graffiti ○ ○

Solutions

a) Ask local businesses to donate trash cans for public areas.
b) Encourage people and businesses to plant trees and plants.
c) Put signs in parks asking people to clean up after their animals.
d) Ask local paint stores to donate paint.
e) Get students to make anti-littering posters.
f) Encourage people to keep pets confined and not let them breed.
g) Ask local businesses to set up recycling centers.
h) Get kids to volunteer to paint attractive murals on walls.
i) Ask vets to provide free sterilizations.
j) Have neighborhood meetings to educate people about recycling.

Define the problems. You've been reading about a hypothetical situation in a hypothetical town. The idea is that the Greenwood project might serve as a model for a real project in a real community – yours.

In groups, follow these steps.

● *Make a list of problems in your town.*
● *Eliminate problems that really cannot be dealt with on a community level (things like air pollution or traffic congestion).*
● *Choose one or two problems to focus on.*

Make a plan. Follow these steps.

● *For the problems you chose to focus on, make a list of possible actions.*
● *Analyze your list and decide which actions are the most realistic.*
● *Explain your plan to the class: We're going to focus on the problem of garbage in the streets and highways. We're going to try to involve people in each of our neighborhoods to educate the public about littering. We'll ask neighborhood schools to let us talk to the children. Maybe local businesses will ...*

[3] Learning check

1 Progress check

a Complete the text with the correct answer from the list below.

On March 1 1836, readers all over Britain (1) ……… for another installment of the latest
work by Charles Dickens. Dickens and his publishers (2) ……… to publish *Pickwick Papers*
in 20 monthly installments. This innovation (3) ……… worked but the public (4) ………
the first installments of the book. Novels had been published in England since the early 18th
century but their potential became apparent with the publication of Sir Walter Scott's *Waverly*
novels in 1814. By the 1830s some 50,000 Britons (5) ……… regular readers of fiction.

1 **a)** waited	**b)** wait	**c)** were waiting	**d)** waiting
2 **a)** were deciding	**b)** decided	**c)** deciding	**d)** had decided
3 **a)** had not	**b)** could not have	**c)** might not have	**d)** must have
4 **a)** were loving	**b)** had loving	**c)** could love	**d)** loved
5 **a)** was	**b)** had been	**c)** were	**d)** were being

b Complete the mind map with four words connected with books.

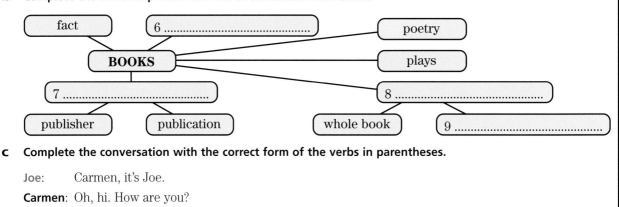

fact   6 …………………………………   poetry

BOOKS   plays

7 …………………………………   8 …………………………………

publisher   publication   whole book   9 …………………………………

c Complete the conversation with the correct form of the verbs in parentheses.

Joe: Carmen, it's Joe.

Carmen: Oh, hi. How are you?

Joe: Fine. Listen, what are you doing on Friday night? My brother's rock group (10) ……………
…………… (play) their first concert. It (11) …………………………… (be) fun!

Carmen: Yeah, sounds fun. But what time?

Joe: Seven.

Carmen: So early! Anyway I can't. I (12) …………………………… (take) an aerobics course then.

Joe: Oh, right. It starts at 6:30. I forgot. You're training to be an instructor, aren't you? How's it going?

Carmen: OK, but it's really hard. Anyway, in three months I (13) …………………………… (finish) it.

Joe: That's not so bad. Hey, come for a quick beer after your class. It's Friday so they
(14) …………………………… (stay) open until midnight, as they always do.

Carmen: Midnight? I don't know. Well, why not! OK, I (15) …………………………… (come), but only for one!

2 Proficiency check

a Listen to six people talking about their future plans and match the subjects in the list to each speaker. Which one is the extra subject?

Speaker 1 ....   a) decorating at home

Speaker 2 ....   b) saving money to buy things

Speaker 3 ....   c) losing weight

Speaker 4 ....   d) making a career change

Speaker 5 ....   e) looking for an apartment

Speaker 6 ....   f) working out

                     g) travelling overseas

Extra subject = ...

b Read the article and choose the correct completion (a–d) for each sentence.

Internet users frequently expect to be able to download information for free. In many cases this isn't a problem but one of the world's most successful websites, Napster, which had over 50 million clients, made it a problem.

Napster was founded in 1998 by a 19-year-old student, Shawn Fanning. It quickly distributed its software around the globe to millions of committed users. Mr. Fanning's software allowed people to share music without paying copyright fees – a development that terrified many industry chiefs. Under the same principle people would be able to share videos, movies and even books in digital form.

In a historic court case, an appeals court in California ruled that the company could no longer knowingly trade in copyrighted material. It also found Napster could be held liable for users of the service who swap copyrighted songs among themselves.

Over the following weekend, millions took advantage of what they feared would be Napster's final hours of existence, exchanging and downloading more than 250 million songs, which would cost millions of dollars to buy on conventional CDs or tapes.

It looked like the end for Napster. But whether Napster ever comes back to life or not, a host of free song-swap services, such as Scour.com and Gnutella are ready to take its place.

1 The problem that Napster highlighted was that:
   a) people expect to be able to download things for free.
   b) anyone, even young people, can set up a website.
   c) software can be distributed around the world.
   d) downloading songs for free breaks copyright law.

2 Napster provided software which:
   a) charged users a small fee for downloading songs.
   b) provided songs and videos free of charge.
   c) allowed users to download songs without any charge.
   d) produced songs and movies for Internet users.

3 Industry chiefs were terrified by Napster's service because:
   a) there were too many users.
   b) they could see the same approach being applied to videos, books, etc.
   c) Shawn Fanning wasn't a member of a record company.
   d) it started to offer movies as well as songs to users.

4 A court in California decided that:
   a) Napster could go on providing music to clients.
   b) Napster had to pay a large fine.
   c) Napster could not continue to provide copyrighted songs to people.
   d) Napster had to stop its service immediately.

5 Lots of people rushed to download songs because:
   a) they wanted to support Napster.
   b) there was a special offer for users.
   c) they were angry about the court's decision.
   d) they were afraid Napster wouldn't be able to continue.

Unit 7 The world of sport

1 Your view

1 Speaking

a Survey. Find people in the class who:

- play a competitive sport (not just do exercise) every week
- have competed in a regional, national or international sports competition
- almost never play any competitive sports but often watch them
- are not interested in either playing or watching sports
- think sports can cause many problems (aggression, injuries, etc.)

> **Language assistant**
>
> Look at these questions about sports: *Do you play any sport? Do you play tennis (soccer, etc.)? Do you swim (ski, etc.)?* Note that *practice* is normally used only for specific training or preparation: *I practice tennis (skiing, etc.) every day.*

b In groups, discuss the results of your survey.

1 Is the class generally pro-sports, anti-sports or divided?
2 Are there more sports participants or spectators?

2 Speaking and reading

a In pairs, discuss how you feel about the sports in the photographs.

b Read the first paragraph of part of an article below. Which of the three sports in the photographs is it about?

"It is the only major sport where the intention is to inflict serious injury on your opponent and we feel that we must have a total ban. For as long as the head is a valid target, brain injuries are going to occur," said Dr. O'Neill. "None of the safety measures that have been introduced over the last ten to twenty years have had any significant impact on the brain injury and eye damage that occur."

c Read the rest of the article. In pairs, discuss whether you agree in general with Dr. O'Neill or with Dr. Warburton.

The British Medical Association (BMA) has been campaigning for a ban on all forms of boxing since 1985. It has sponsored legislation in parliament to try to get the sport abolished. The BMA also commissioned a 60-second movie theater advertisement in 1996 which won three awards.

However, the organization's policy has been criticized by some in the medical world. Dr. Nigel Warburton, a professor of philosophy, argued in the Journal of Medical Ethics that the policy is "inconsistent, paternalistic and too weak to justify a change to criminal law." He said that between 1986 and 1992 boxing accounted for three deaths in England and Wales compared with 77 deaths from motor sports, 69 from air sports, 54 from mountain climbing, 40 from ball games and 28 from horseback riding.

The BMA responded by claiming that Dr. Warburton's article underplayed the "chronic brain damage caused by boxing, a factor which is not generally present in other sports."

J Med Ethics 1998; 24(1); 56-60, with permission from the BMT Publishing Group

d In pairs, list arguments for and against boxing. As a whole class, have a debate on whether to ban boxing or not in your country. Elect a chairperson to control the debate and give everyone the opportunity to express their opinion. Then vote and see if the majority is for or against a ban on boxing.

3 Word builder: the body and sports

a In pairs, identify the parts of the body in the box and match them with the photograph. Use a dictionary if necessary.

> ankle calf elbow heel jaw knee
> neck rib shoulder thigh toe wrist

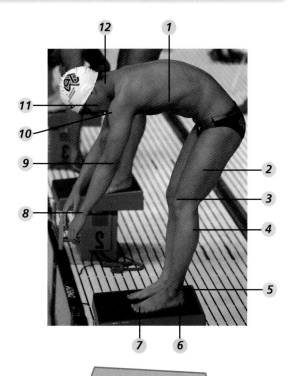

b Which of the parts of the body above, and others, might you *break* or *fracture*, *twist* or *sprain*, *dislocate* or *bruise*? Have you had any sports injuries of these kinds?

c What parts of the body do you use to *catch*, *dribble*, *hit*, *hold*, *jump*, *kick*, *row* and *throw* with?

You row a boat with your arms.

4 Listening and speaking

a You are going to hear a TV show called *What's my Sport?* Contestants ask the athletes (hidden and with disguised voices) up to 12 *yes / no* questions to guess their sports. Listen to the first eight questions. Try to guess the sport and the person.

b Listen to the answers.

c Play *What's my Sport?*

Learning tip

When learning new words, note the contexts they are used in – the other words around them and the grammar, e.g. *sprain*: I **sprained** <u>my ankle</u> when I fell, or *break*: He **broke** <u>his arm</u> playing soccer. (injury + possessive + part of body). This helps you remember the word and its appropriate use. Write three sentences combining words from exercises 3a, b and c above.

2 The business view

1 Speaking

a What do these headlines have in common? What is your reaction to them?

b Can you name the following? If you can't, try to find the answers from other people.

1 the sports Shaquille O'Neal, Luis Figo and Alex Rodriguez play
2 the American city where the Lakers are based
3 the Spanish team Luis Figo moved to
4 the sport that pays top players most

2 Reading and speaking

a Read the article and answer the questions. Discuss your answers in pairs.

1 According to economists, are top athletes worth the millions they earn?
2 What is so special about Shaquille O'Neal?
3 Is the income of NBA teams increasing much?
4 Why can NBA teams calculate their costs better than most businesses?

ARE THEY WORTH IT?

One hundred and twenty-three million dollars for seven years of Shaquille O'Neal, $30 million for one year of Michael Jordan. That's what NBA teams were paying back in 1996. Can anyone be worth that much to put a ball through a hoop? The answer is yes ... the way economists keep score. It's a simple case of supply and demand.

For example, the supply of 7-foot-1-inch, 300-pound giants is extremely limited, especially ones like Shaq, who can move with extraordinary agility for his size. On the other hand, the money provided by television networks and ticket buyers is expanding fast and good teams get a bigger slice of the cake. Team quality generates demand, and demand determines ticket prices. The better the team, the more intense the demand for a fixed number of seats. And that's why stars are worth so much, says economist and sports expert Roger Noll of Stanford University.

The whole NBA takes in more than $3 billion annually, and it is becoming as popular in places like Zagreb, Croatia as it is in Chicago. More important, unlike many businesses, basketball team owners know what their costs will be over the next few years. The players get 48% of the league's basketball-related income and each team has a salary cap of $35.5 million. So a team that brings in $70 million has plenty of money left after "labor costs."

b Find expressions that mean the same as:

1 score a basket
2 market forces
3 make more money
4 outstanding players
5 top limit on payroll
6 salary expenses

c In groups, discuss whether **anyone** (sports star, president, etc.) should make $30 million a year, and whether other people (doctors, teachers, etc.) should make more than they usually do.

3 Grammar builder: review and extension of relative clauses

a Work in pairs. How do we use *who*, *which* and *that* for people and things in relative clauses? Use these examples to help you.

1 *Soccer is a sport **which** most men and many women like.*
2 *Baseball is the sport **that** pays top players most.*
3 *Phil Jackson is the coach **who** made the Chicago Bulls six-time NBA champions.*
4 *Michael Jordan is the great player **that** Jackson needed to win the league.*

b Decide which of the sentences in exercise 3a can omit *who*, *which* or *that*.

*O'Neal is the player **(that)** the Lakers bought for $123 million.*

c Now examine the following sentences. What happens in the second, more common type? Write more sentences like it, using the ideas below.

*Real Madrid is the team **to which** Figo moved.* →
*Real Madrid is the team Figo moved **to**.*

1 Portugal is the country ....(Figo comes from Portugal.)
2 O'Neal is the player .... (The Lakers paid $123 million for him.)
3 Baseball is the game ....(Most Americans are crazy about it.)

4 Pronunciation: weak form of *that*

a Listen to the sentences below. Practice the weak *that* and the flow of the "noun + *that* + verb" phrase.

Baseball is <u>the sport that pays most</u>. Soccer's <u>a game that's played everywhere</u>.
He was <u>the player that made them champions</u>.

b In pairs, give your choice of:

1 a sports star who is a good example for young people.
2 a sports star who is a disgrace.
3 a sport that should be prohibited.

I think bull fighting is a sport that ...

5 Speaking and writing

a There is much more money than stars' salaries in sports – clothing, equipment, fan clubs, and so on, are also big business. In groups, organize a survey to find out how much people spend on sports annually. Design a questionnaire to collect information, with questions like these.

Approximately how much do you spend on sports clothing each year?
Did you have any medical expenses because of sports injuries last year? If so, how much?

b After completing the questionnaire and analyzing the results, compare the results of each group.

3 The career view

1 Reading and speaking

a Read this letter to a magazine. In pairs, discuss each argument or example the writer gives about the difficulty of being successful as a professional athlete.

b Discuss these questions in groups.

1 Who are the most successful professional athletes in your country?

2 Do they all make a lot of money?

3 Are there other athletes who have been famous but have had serious problems?

2 Grammar builder: more relative clauses and modifying phrases

a In pairs, discuss the pairs of sentences below. What is the difference between (a) and (b) in each pair? Check your ideas with the Language assistant.

1 **a)** *It is worse for players,* **who only have a job for a short time,** *than for referees or coaches.*

 b) *It is worse for players* **that only have a job for a short time** *than for those with a long career.*

2 **a)** *I work in semi-professional leagues,* **which have a low stress level,** *not in fully professional leagues.*

 b) *I work in semi-professional leagues* **that have a low stress level**, *not in the ones where stress is high.*

b Convert the two sentences into a single sentence, type a or b, using the pronouns in parentheses.

1 I play soccer whenever I can. It's my favorite sport. (which)

2 This is the boy. He partners me at tennis. (who)

3 The team is at the bottom of the league. It beat us last week. (which)

4 The Spartans won the game. They practice a lot. (who)

5 Refereeing is a profession. It can bring in enough money. (that)

NOT ALL BIG MONEY

Dear Sir,

Don Flynn's article "The Money Game" gives an inaccurate picture of the professional sports world. For every star earning $1 million, there are hundreds or thousands playing full-time for little money or part-time for less. The same may be true for coaches, referees and other sports workers, but it is worse for players, who only have a job for a decade or so.

Young talents hoping to become rich and famous should consider other occupations if they have a good head. Of the nineteen youngsters I coached for a famous soccer team ten years ago, only four are still playing, and only two on the first team, both as reserves. Professional sports offer most players a strenuous, disappointing, poorly-paid and short professional career, often even shorter because of injury.

Incidentally, I am now a qualified soccer referee. I work mostly in semi-professional leagues, which have a low stress level, not in fully professional soccer, where stress is high. I earn enough to provide for myself and my family decently, and a colleague is still refereeing at age 61.

Yours, James Sinclair

Language assistant

1 Some relative clauses define or specify the person or thing we are talking about, e.g. *players* **who only have a job for a short time** or *players* **that have a long career**. These are defining clauses and *that* may be used instead of *who* or *which*.

2 Some relative clauses just give extra information about a person or thing, e.g. *players,* **who only have a job for a short time** or *referees,* **who can have long careers**. These are non-defining clauses. They are separated from the rest of the sentence by commas and *who* or *which* must be used (not *that*). They are uncommon in speech, but often used in writing.

c Look at other ways that we use to modify nouns. Then write the sentences below in a different way.

*The woman **who is wearing red** is the champion.*

*The woman **wearing red** is the champion.*

*The woman **dressed in red** is the champion.*

*The woman **in red** is the champion.*

1   The new player that was bought by United is only 16.

  The new player .... is only 16.

2   The Italian who is now managing Rangers is very experienced.

  The Italian .... is very experienced.

3   The woman who is sitting in the armchair was the Wimbledon singles champion in the 1960s.

  The woman .... was the Wimbledon singles champion in the 1960s.

3 Speaking and listening

a Anna Kournikova is a young tennis star who, after years as a professional, has never won a major singles championship. However, she earns a lot of money. In pairs, note ways she might earn money without winning major tournaments.

b Listen to a radio talk and check your ideas about how Anna Kournikova makes money.

c Imagine you have a daughter of about ten who shows extraordinary talent at tennis and has won every national girls' tournament. An American coach based in Florida has offered to prepare her for international competition, assuring you that she will make an absolute fortune. In groups, discuss what you would do.

LANGUAGE for life:

the REALLY big

sports festival

1 The Olympic Games

We always seem to be recovering from or preparing for the Olympic Games – the Summer Olympics, that is. But do you actually know much about them?

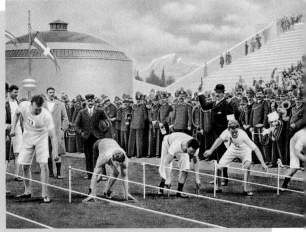

Test yourself with this quiz.

1 When were the very first ancient Olympic Games held?
   a) 776 BC.   b) 76 BC.   c) 776 AD.

2 Where were they held?
   a) In Egypt.   b) In Greece.   c) In Rome.

3 What nationality was the person who created the modern Olympic Games?
   a) English.   b) American.   c) French.

4 When were the first modern Olympic Games?
   a) 1806   b) 1896   c) 1906

5 How many athletes participated in those Games?
   a) 145   b) 245   c) 450

6 How many athletes participated in the Sydney 2000 Games?
   a) About 2,500.   b) About 5,000.   c) About 10,000.

7 What does the five-ring symbol represent?
   a) The original five sports.   b) The five continents.   c) The five cities of ancient Greece.

8 Can you name the venue for the 2004 Olympic Games?
   a) Alexandria, Egypt.   b) Rome, Italy.   c) Athens, Greece.

Now read on and check how much you know.

Beginning in 776 BC, the Olympic Games were held in the valley of Olympia in Greece every four years for almost 1,200 years. Inspired by the ancient Games, Frenchman Baron Pierre de Coubertin created the modern Olympic Games. First staged in 1896, they attracted about 245 athletes (all men) in 43 events. At the Sydney 2000 Games, more than 10,000 athletes took part in 300 events. The Olympic Movement has survived wars, boycotts and terrorism to become a symbol of the ability of the people of all nations to come together in peace and friendship. The five overlapping rings are intended to represent the linking of the five continents. Recent Games have been held on four of those continents (Seoul, Korea, 1988; Barcelona, Spain, 1992; Atlanta, USA, 1996; and Sydney, Australia, 2000), and the 2004 Games are to be in the spiritual home of the Olympics, Athens.

Well, now you know. But just think of all the changes from Athens 1896 to nowadays, e.g. the number of athletes, number and type of sports, the fact that the athletes can now be professional rather than amateur, nationalistic competitiveness, testing for drugs and so on.

Do you think it has been mostly progress and improvement or have some things deteriorated?

② The Olympic objectives

Baron de Coubertin believed the Olympic Games movement could bring nations together in sports and reduce the risk of war. That was his main objective. If you were participating in the organization of the Olympic Games in your country, what would your objectives be, both international and national?

Write a list of five or more objectives.

Well, the Athens 2004 Organizing Committee produced their list of objectives. Listen and see how far they coincide with yours.

③ Where next?

The following cities were the candidates for the 2008 Olympic games: Beijing, Istanbul, Osaka, Paris, Toronto.

Do you know which one won? Which one would you have selected and why?

The following Summer Olympics will be in 2012. Which city would be a good choice for that date? One way of testing opinions is to make proposals and then vote – but **not** for the city you proposed.

Form a group of six and propose a city from a different continent or region: Europe, Asia, Australasia, North America, South America, Africa. Africa is an interesting case: some people say it is time for the Olympics or the World Cup to be in Africa, but a major problem is the enormous investment required.

④ Your chance!

Win tickets to the next Games!

Yes, tickets for two to the next Games, all expenses paid! Just write an essay of 140 to 160 words on "Why the Olympics are a good idea." Don't forget Baron Pierre de Coubertin's original ideas, but you must have ideas of your own too.

The entries will be examined by a panel of sporting experts. The best entrant will win two tickets – all expenses paid!

Remember, competing is the important thing ... but you might even be a winner!

Unit 8 The image industry

1 Making faces

1 Word builder: the human face

a Write the letters of the appropriate parts of the face in the circles.

a) cheek	**d)** eyebrow	**g)** forehead
b) chin	**e)** eyelashes	**h)** lip
c) ear lobe	**f)** eyelid	**i)** nostril

b Complete the paragraph with the appropriate parts of the face.

Marlene uses blush on her (1) .... and she puts heavy gloss on her (2) .... (she uses gloss, not lipstick). She plucks her (3) .... so they're very thin and she wears blue eye shadow and long false (4) ....

Herman shaves, but he has a very small beard on his (5) .... and a mustache on his upper (6) .... He wears a ring in his left (7) .... and another in his right (8) ....

2 Speaking and listening

a In pairs, look at the made-up faces. Student A describe a face and Student B guess which one it is. (Do **not** use *he / she* in your descriptions; use *This face / person* ...)

b Listen to part of a talk. Which of the faces is it related to? In pairs, discuss some of the things you understood from the talk.

c Read the following incomplete notes on the talk and fill in what you can. Then listen again and check. In groups, compare and complete your notes.

1 The Wodaabe people are nomads that live ....

2 With the Wodaabe, it is the .... who try to make themselves attractive to the ....

3 They prepare themselves carefully for their festivals, for example, they:
- shave hair at front of head to make their forehead higher. ....
- ....
- paint lips black to make teeth look whiter. ....
- ....

4 When they are ready, they practice ....

5 In the festivals, a romance usually begins when ....

d In groups, discuss what the men and women you know do to make themselves more attractive.

3 Reading, speaking and writing

a Read this letter to Karla Lightborn, an advice columnist. In pairs, discuss the girl's situation and the advice that Karla could give her.

Dear Karla,

I'm a 16-year-old high school student and I live at home. My parents are very conservative and I'm not allowed to wear much makeup. Well, they don't actually stop me, but they look very unhappy and disapproving when I wear more than the minimum. That wasn't much of a problem until I got my first serious boyfriend this year.

He likes really attractive girls and although I'm no great beauty, I can look good when I'm made up and dressed to impress. When he sees me without makeup, like when I haven't had time to make myself up before leaving home, he laughs at me. That's when he's in a good mood. When he's in a bad mood, he groans and looks disgusted.

What can I do about this conflict? I really do love and respect my parents, but I love my boyfriend too and want him to be proud of me. All the girls are attracted to him because he's excellent at sports and really good-looking. He's intelligent too. In fact, he and I usually get the best grades in our class. If I don't look beautiful enough for him, I'm afraid he'll leave me for some other girl.

Please help me.

"Plain Desperate," New Jersey

b Individually, write a reply to "Plain Desperate," in three main paragraphs. Consider the following and start like the example.

Paragraph 1: Her relationship with her parents.
Should she continue doing what they want or do what she wants?
Paragraph 2: Her relationship with her first serious boyfriend.
Does he really love and respect her, or just want to be with glamorous girls? Does she really love him, or just want to be with one of the most attractive boys?
Paragraph 3: The kind of relationship she should seek for the long term.
Should she value looks more than character and behavior or character and behavior more than looks?

Dear "Desperate,"

Your situation is more common than you imagine. I think you should consider three things: your relationship with your parents, the reality of the relationship between you and your boyfriend and your own long-term future.

First, let's consider your relationship with your parents. You are 16 and ...

c In groups, read one another's letters and vote for the one with the best and clearest advice.

d Discuss whether there are many parents and many boyfriends like "Desperate's."

2 Cosmetic surgery

1 Word builder: medicine

a Complete the text with phrases from the box. Then use each phrase in an appropriate form (e.g. past tense) in a sentence. Compare your sentences in groups.

> do operations   operate on
> have an operation   was operated on

Last year, my mother decided to (1) ……………………… to remove the wrinkles from her face. Her brother did it. He's a plastic surgeon, and he has to (2) ……………………… like that every day. Mom (3) ……………………… in his office, which saved the cost of an operating room. Now Mom looks younger than me, with a fantastic complexion! My uncle will probably (4) ……………………… me soon for my 29th birthday.

Language assistant

You can not say ~~He operated me~~ / ~~I was operated.~~ You have to say *He operated on me / I was operated on.*

b Complete the text with words from the box. Use a dictionary if necessary.

> appointment   cure   heal   prescription   scar   stitches   treatment   wound

The (1) …………… was at 11:30. Dr. Browning called me in right on time. She assured me there was a simple (2) …………… for the car accident (3) …………… that twisted my mouth. Very soon she had made a single incision and drawn it together with tiny (4) …………… . She gave me a (5) …………… for a cream to help the incision (6) …………… without leaving a (7) …………… . It really worked. I strongly recommend Dr. Browning for that kind of (8) …………… .

Learning tip

To understand and learn vocabulary, you often need to use several strategies together, e.g. noting similarities with words in your own language, noting context, and checking in your dictionary. For example, there may be words in your language similar to *complexion* and *cure*, but the context may suggest that the English words have a different meaning. Check these words in your dictionary again. Is the meaning the same?

c In groups, discuss your own, your relatives' and your friends' experiences with medical treatment.

2 Speaking and reading

a In pairs, exchange opinions about these two photographs. Who would you prefer as your grandparents and why? Who would you prefer to be like when you are a grandparent and why?

b Read the article about cosmetic surgery. Some of the information is missing. Complete it with figures from the box.

| 15 | under 19s | 25% | 30 |
| 150% | 100,000 | 1,000,000 | |

Once it was only rich and famous women "of a certain age" that had cosmetic surgery, and they were operated on in secret. But now society is generally more conscious of image and people of all ages – and both genders – are openly improving on what nature gave them.

Between 1990 and 1999 cosmetic surgery procedures increased more than (1) .... Almost (2) .... procedures were performed on women in 1998 and about (3) .... on men. The most common procedure for (4) .... is nose-reshaping. After that age, a whole range of face and body procedures are common. In fact, (5) .... of cosmetic surgery patients are repeat patients.

The trend is not just in the United States. In *The Masks of Argentina,* author Luis Majul estimates that one in every (6) .... Argentines has undergone cosmetic surgery – Diego Maradona and ex-President Carlos Menem are included in that number. Many girls of (7) .... or more from Mexico through Europe and Japan are given cosmetic surgery in exchange for promises to get better grades in school. Most get new noses or new thighs, but the same old grades.

c In groups, discuss the benefits and problems you have heard about that result from cosmetic surgery (e.g. nose reshaping, facelifts, liposuction and breast implants).

3 Grammar builder: review and extension of passives

Complete the second sentence in each pair so that it means approximately the same as the first one. Check in pairs.

There were over 1,000,000 cosmetic procedures performed in 1998.

Over 1,000,000 cosmetic procedures **were performed** in 1998.

1 All the girls are attracted to him. He .... all the girls.
2 My uncle will operate on thirty women next month.
   Thirty women .... by my uncle next month.
3 Several new surgical techniques have been introduced this year.
   They .... this year.
4 Doctors can legally do minor surgery in their offices.
   Minor surgery .... in doctors' offices.
5 More people are using cosmetic surgery now.
   Cosmetic surgery .... more people now.

4 Speaking

Complete **one** of these sentences.

- I would never have cosmetic surgery because ...
- I would have cosmetic surgery if ...
   In groups, read your sentences out loud and discuss them.

> **Language assistant**
> Remember that the passive is used more in formal language (especially writing) than in informal language (especially conversation). Also, it moves the main focus of attention from the doer (if specified) to the receiver.
> *A surgeon reduced the size of my nose.* ➤ *The size of my nose was reduced (by a surgeon).*
> surgeon = doer
> size of my nose = receiver

3 Selling beauty

1 Speaking

a Examine these advertisements. In pairs, discuss the different strategies used to try to get people to buy each product.

b Discuss these questions.

- What specific advertisements can you remember (e.g. from magazines, on TV, on billboards in the streets)?
- Why do you remember them?
- Do you buy any of the products they promote?

2 Listening and speaking

a You are going to hear a radio interview about beauty products. Before you listen, decide if you think these statements are true (T) or false (F).

1 Cosmetics experts perform operations. T ○ F ○
2 Most beauty products would not sell without advertising. T ○ F ○
3 In the past, some beauty products killed women. T ○ F ○
4 The FDA* has a very strict control over beauty products. T ○ F ○
5 Allergies to beauty products are not a widespread problem. T ○ F ○
6 Beauty products have a generally beneficial effect. T ○ F ○

*FDA = Food and Drug Administration (U.S.)

b Look up the word *lead* (a metal) in a dictionary. Listen and check your answers to exercise 2a.

c Listen again and discuss these questions in groups.

1 What does the man mean by "Beauty care is high on the human agenda almost everywhere?"
2 What does he mean by problem-solving products and beauty-enhancing products?

d In groups, discuss your own answers to the woman's questions.

- Would most beauty products sell without the enormous amount of advertising they receive?
- Do many beauty products have harmful effects?
- Do many beauty products provoke allergic reactions?
- Do most beauty products have a beneficial effect?

3 Pronunciation: intonation – questions

a Listen to these questions. Does the intonation go up or down on the underlined syllable? Mark each main intonation change ↑ or ↓.

1 Who's your favorite <u>ac</u>tress?

2 Does she use a lot of <u>make</u>up?

3 Why are men spending more on personal <u>care</u> products?

4 Are men as vain as <u>wo</u>men?

b Which questions go up and which go down: those beginning with question words (e.g. *who, what, why*) or those beginning with verbs (e.g. *does, has, are*)?

c Listen again and copy the intonation. Then ask each other the questions.

4 Grammar builder: active and passive

Read the following memo about a product promotion. Complete the text with the appropriate forms, active or passive, of the verbs in parentheses.

FROM: Jack Halstrom
TO: Sally Martin
SUBJECT: Lip-Glo promotion

Hi, Sally. I (1) .... (almost finish) the promotion report. I (2) .... (have) it to you at least an hour before the meeting tomorrow. For your information, the main points (3) .... (summarize) below.
Jack

Last week, Laura Glen (4) .... (employ) to make a series of five new TV commercials. ProMo Studios (5) .... (have) them ready for next month. These commercials (6) .... (show) on all major channels in the afternoon right through the fall, winter and spring. Stills from the commercials (7) .... (use) in new magazine advertisements.

New packaging for Lip-Glo (8) .... (design) at the moment. It (9) .... (go) into production next month, and it (10) .... (be) in the stores just before the TV campaign (11) .... (begin) in the fall.

The retail price of Lip-Glo (12) .... (reduce) by 10% to coincide with the beginning of the TV campaign. Sales (13) .... (expect) to rise by at least 25% during the campaign and the increase should (14) .... (sustain) for a good period after that.

5 Speaking and writing

a Imagine your team has to present a new product proposal to the Board of a beauty products company. Plan the presentation, considering these points.

- the type of product, e.g. a cream to eliminate wrinkles around the eyes
- the proposed name of the product, e.g. "Lovely Look"
- the market segment it is aimed at, e.g. women between the ages of 30 and 50
- the promotion strategy proposed, e.g. TV commercials and women's magazine advertisements

b Present your team's proposal to "the Board" (the class). After listening to all the different teams' proposals, vote for the best one.

LANGUAGE for life:
advertising *and promotion*

① Carrying the message

② Jingle, jingle, little ad

Both these scenes show people promoting products or services. But there's an enormous difference between them, isn't there? Why on earth did people use to walk around the streets with advertising boards? Well, there could be some very good reasons. Can you think of some?

And those kids – why on earth would they want to wear sweatshirts promoting the manufacturer? Well, again you can think of some reasons, can't you? (You yourself may be advertising something at this moment without being paid for it – check your clothes and possessions!)

So, what do you think? Are people being exploited by business more nowadays than ever before? If so, is that a good or a bad thing? Where will it end?

Are you a jingle addict? Do you sing the catchy songs promoting a breakfast cereal, a toothpaste or a detergent? Obviously, a lot of people work in the business of slogan and copy writing. And the best can make a lot of money for little work. Could it be a job for you?

Think of as many jingles and slogans as you can. What makes them memorable? Now, can you come up with a good jingle or a slogan for a product or service in your country or community? Here is one for an imaginary product as an example.

When you're hot, RicaCola is really cool.

When you're cool, RicaCola is what lets everyone know.

③ Learning the profession

Advertising and promotion doesn't just consist of clever ideas. A real marketing professional needs to know many technical concepts and procedures. That means studying. How would you manage as a marketing student with texts like this one?

Read it and check yourself by matching the following statements with Ogilvy's six principles.

a) Make your advertisements really interesting.

b) Be original in your thinking and approach advertising in new ways.

c) Don't do cheap, second-rate advertising that will reflect poorly on your product.

d) Right at the start, decide what market sector you are aiming at.

e) Don't get into detail, but just push a single viable idea.

f) Present your product as something very different and much better than any other.

KEYS TO ADVERTISING SUCCESS

Often the business of advertising is so complex that students and advertisers alike wring their hands and cry, "Just give me a few simple rules for an effective ad campaign."

In an advertisement (appropriately enough) in the *Wall Street Journal*, David Ogilvy of Ogilvy & Mather, one of the nation's top advertising firms, listed 38 pointers to the way of success in creating a good advertising campaign. Here are a few that are common to all advertisements, regardless of the medium:

1 The most important decision is how to position your product in the market. Make that decision before you plan your campaign.

2 Make the promises in your campaign unique and competitive. In the 18th century, Dr. Johnson said: "Promise, large promise, is the soul of an advertisement."

3 Don't be a bore. Nobody was ever bored into buying a product.

4 Innovate. Start trends instead of following them.

5 Reduce your strategy to one central promise and go all the way in delivering that promise.

6 It pays to give most products an image of quality and the advertisements should reflect that image.

These are some of the principles Ogilvy uses in creating advertising for his clients. As his company has created more than several billions of dollars of advertising, it seems safe to conclude that his formulas have been successful.

④ Promotion

Imagine you have an important advertising agency. Two foreign companies approach you about the introduction of their products in your country. Listen and note the product of each customer.

CUSTOMER 1

PRODUCT ....

MORE INFORMATION ....

....

....

CUSTOMER 2

PRODUCT ....

MORE INFORMATION ....

....

....

Now listen again and note some more information about the products.

What would you tell each customer about the prospects of their product in your country and how to approach the promotion? With a classmate (your business partner!) plan what would you say. Then practice, with one of you as yourself and the other as a customer. Yes, practice! You can't be too careful with contracts that might be worth millions of dollars!

4 Learning check

1 Progress check

a Complete the sentences with the correct word (a–c).

1 That's the team ……… was relegated to last place this season.
   a) which   **b)** who   **c)** whose

2 Marion's the first member of our club ……… won a chess tournament.
   a) which   **b)** whose   **c)** who

3 Manchester United is the soccer team ……… makes most money.
   a) that   **b)** who   **c)** whose

4 Wimbledon is the place ……… the All England Tennis Championship takes place.
   a) which   **b)** where   **c)** when

5 Tony's the player ……… they accused of taking drugs last year.
   a) which   **b)** whose   **c)** – (no pronoun)

b Read the first sentence of each pair. Complete the second sentence of each pair so it has the same meaning.

6 More cosmetic products are being bought by men these days.
   These days men …………………… more cosmetic products.

7 A lot of people are influenced by television advertising of products.
   Television advertising of products …………………… a lot of people.

8 Most governments have introduced laws to protect consumers.
   Laws to protect consumers …………………………………………… by most governments.

9 Cosmetic companies sell a lot of beauty products on the Internet.
   A lot of beauty products …………………… on the Internet.

10 Huge quantities of fake cosmetics were confiscated by the police last year.
    The police …………………… huge quantities of fake cosmetics last year.

11 Cosmetics companies will spend millions of dollars on promotion next year.
    Millions of dollars …………………… on promotion next year by cosmetic companies.

c Complete the sentences with the best word from the box.

prescription	healed	scar	cured	wound	surgery	receipt	operation

12 Mick cut his leg but fortunately it ………………… very quickly.

13 I fell off my bike when I was a kid and still have a ………………… on my arm.

14 A lot of people have cosmetic ………………… to try and make themselves look more attractive.

15 In most countries you need a doctor's ………………… to get antibiotics.

2 Proficiency check

a Listen to this radio news broadcast and complete the paragraph with appropriate words or figures from the broadcast.

Frenchman Michel Desjoyeux was the winner of the Vendée Globe yacht race in March 2001, but you would be forgiven for believing that it was, in fact, won by a diminutive Englishwoman. There was far more excitement about the person who won (1) .... place, Ellen MacArthur. Ellen is now both the fastest and the (2) .... Briton to sail around the world: she is just (3) .... years old and she weighs only (4) .... kilos. The Vendée Globe race covers 38,500 kilometers across four oceans in the most difficult (5) .... imaginable. Ellen completed the race in (6) .... days, but on her way she experienced extremely dangerous incidents such as coming face to face with a huge (7) ....! Ellen wrote 2,500 letters to get enough (8) .... to compete in the race but could now attract offers of around $150,000 to write the book of her journey.

b Read this newspaper article. Four sentences have been removed from it. Choose the most suitable sentence below. There is one extra sentence.

a) During that period it circled the earth more than 80,000 times, at a cost of $218 million a year.

b) During the Cold War, military testing was carried out on Mir.

c) The most serious occurred on June 25, 1997, when a progress supply ship crashed into the station, almost sending it out of control.

d) It also helped scientists learn about the difficulties of spending longer periods of time in space.

e) Up to 50 tons of debris, some as big as a small car, plunged into the sea hundreds of miles southeast of Fiji.

On March 23 2001 the Mir space station crashed safely into the South Pacific. (1) .... Most of the 150-ton spacecraft burned up as it reentered the atmosphere.

Mir was launched on February 20, 1986. Its original lifespan was intended to be just three to five years, but it was in orbit for 15 years. (2) ....

The space station consisted of six modules, providing habitation, laboratory and storage facilities. To make crew members feel at home there were carpets, colored walls and furniture. Soyuz aircraft were used to transport crews to and from the station. Mir played host to 44 expeditions and around 23,000 scientific experiments. (3) .... One crew member, Valeri Polyakov, stayed aboard a record 439 days.

During the 1990s, Mir was plagued by mishaps. (4) .... Days later there was another emergency when Mir's main computer was accidentally disconnected, causing the station to start spinning and threatening a catastrophic loss of power.

Unit 9 A question of luck

1 Good and bad luck

> **superstition** *n.* a belief in the existence or power of the supernatural; irrational fear of the unknown

1 Speaking and reading

What is superstition? Discuss your ideas in groups and then read the definition.

2 Listening and speaking

a Listen to the interview and check (✔) the items which the speaker mentions. Are they lucky or unlucky? Write L or U in the second circles.

b Listen to the interview again and answer the questions.

1 Why are black cats thought to be unlucky?
2 What do many people do if they spill some salt?
3 What examples of good luck charms does the interviewer mention?
4 What unlucky things does the interviewer mention?

c Work in groups of three or four. Do any of these superstitions exist in your country? Do you know any superstitions from other countries? Describe them to your group.

3 Word builder: affixes

Affixes can be used to form verbs from other words.

prefixes: *define – **re**define, like – **dis**like, hear – **over**hear, understand – **mis**understand*

suffixes: *energy – energ**ize**, sweet – sweet**en**, alien – alien**ate***

Write a suitable verb in each sentence. Use the word in bold and one of the affixes above.

1 My pencil's blunt. I need to ....it. **sharp**
2 The company needs to .... its operations to compete. **computer**
3 If airlines .... and you can't get your seat, they must give compensation. **book**
4 After the earthquake, the government had to .... large areas of the city. **build**
5 In marketing you have to be able to .... your products. **different**
6 Political rivals tried to .... the opposition's name. **black**

4 Pronunciation: intonation – lists

a **Listen to this list from the interview in exercise 2 and notice the intonation.**

Lots of people use the image of a saint,↑ *a crucifix*↑ *or something similar.*↓

b **Say these sentences and mark the intonation on them. Then listen and check your answers. Practice the intonation.**

1 For my birthday I got a sweater, two CDs and a pen.
2 It was a great lunch: we had fish chowder, salmon, salad and blueberry pie.
3 Unlucky things include breaking mirrors, leaving keys on tables and even wearing gold and silver together.

5 Reading and writing

a **Work in pairs. What do these pictures all have in common? Student A read paragraphs 1 and 2 about Friday 13th. Student B read paragraph 3 about Apollo 13. Then exchange information about your paragraphs. Finally, both read paragraphs 4 and 5 and talk about the main ideas.**

ARE YOU A TRISKAIDEKAPHOBIC?

1 Do you know what *triskaidekaphobia* is? Well, it is a fear of the number 13. Why are we so obsessed with 13 being unlucky?

2 According to some experts, the "evil" connection between Friday and the 13th may have its roots with the presence of 13 people at the Last Supper, and Christ's subsequent crucifixion on Good Friday. Since then, when Friday is combined with the number 13, it is supposed to bring a double dose of misfortune.

3 Past disasters linked to the number 13 hardly help triskaidekaphobics overcome their affliction. The most famous is the Apollo 13 mission: Apollo 13 left from Pad 39 (three times 13) at 13:13 local time. It was launched on April 11, 1970: 4 (April is the fourth month of the year) + 11 + 70 = 85; 8 + 5 = 13. Finally, it was struck by disaster on April 13, when one of its oxygen tanks exploded.

4 Famous triskaidekaphobics include Napoleon, Mark Twain and the German composer Richard Wagner. Several key events in Wagner's life – including his birth in 1813 and death (February 13, 1883) were linked to the number 13. U.S. President Franklin Roosevelt was a particularly severe case. He would cancel any lunch or dinner with 13 people round the table. He also avoided going on visits on the 13th of the month.

5 Maybe it's just a superstition but how many buildings have you seen with a 13th floor or hotels with a room 13? Why take a chance?

b **Are there any things which you consider very lucky or unlucky? Write a paragraph about something you think is lucky or unlucky, and why.**

2 Optimism versus pessimism

1 Speaking

a Discuss these sayings in groups of three. Are they optimistic or pessimistic?

Look on the bright side.

You can't beat the system.

It never rains but it pours.

Life isn't fair.

Don't worry, be happy.

Tomorrow's another day.

b Which two do you think reflect your philosophy best?

2 Reading

a Read the two texts (below and opposite) quickly and answer the question.

What kind of text is each one: a story, an advertisement, a newspaper article or a report?

b Read the texts again. Which text does each statement reflect, A, B or both?

1 Too much pressure on people to be happy may be negative. ....
2 It is important to complain sometimes. ....
3 A lot of self-help books try to make us feel optimistic. ....
4 Self-help books don't work all the time. ....
5 Being pessimistic can help us deal with difficult situations. ....

A

Stop Smiling, Start Kvetching: A 5-Step Guide to Creative Complaining
By Barbara Held, Ph.D.

If you are tired of being told: "Cheer up – things could be worse," "Smile – look on the bright side," "Stop complaining – it's not that bad." If you have ever said to yourself: "What's to stop things from getting worse?" "The bright side isn't that bright," "Why should I stop complaining – it is pretty bad." Then you need to assert your inalienable right to *kvetch* ("complain" in Yiddish) – and this book will show you how.

Self-help books abound. And virtually every one of them pushes us to look on the bright side – to be ever more optimistic, cheerful, positive, happy. If this "don't worry, be happy" approach to life worked, would we need so many of these self-help books? Aren't there times when you feel miserable about something and just want to complain about it?

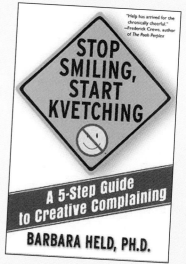

PUBLISHER: St Martin's Griffin
ISBN: 0-312-28351-2 © 2001
PRICE: $9.95

B

Always looking on the bright side can damage your health, American psychologists believe. Meeting at their annual conference, they attacked what they termed "the tyranny of the positive attitude": the kind of relentless optimism preached by American self-help gurus, business managers and religious leaders. A symposium at the American Psychological Association conference decided to recommend "the overlooked virtues of negativity."

A growing band of psychologists believes that the pressure to be cheerful glosses over a person's need for a good moan every so often and may make some people depressed.

Dr. Julie Norem, a social psychologist at Wellesley college in Massachussetts, has produced a study on "defensive pessimism". This involves people setting absurdly low expectations for themselves to help master difficult situations. Preparing for an interview, for example, the optimist imagines only the best outcome, whereas the defensive pessimist thinks of tripping over the carpet, spilling the coffee, garbling answers. If he or she fears the worst, the pessimist devises means to avoid it: by wearing low shoes rather than heels, by refusing coffee when offered and being thoroughly prepared with answers.

3 Grammar builder: real and unreal conditionals

a Look at the examples of conditionals and write the numbers in the appropriate column of the table.

1 If he or she fears the worst, the pessimist devises means to avoid it.
2 If I had lots of money, I'd probably buy a sports car.
3 You'll see a lot of advice about being positive if you read self-help books.
4 If I were you, I'd stop smoking.
5 If I weren't a pessimist, I might have more friends.

Open / Real conditionals	Hypothetical / Unreal conditionals

b Match the sentences in exercise 3a with the definitions.

a) Talking about an improbable or imaginary situation in the present or future. ◯
b) Talking about something that is always or usually true. ◯
c) Giving advice. ◯
d) Talking about an impossible or imaginary situation in the present. ◯
e) Talking about a situation which is possible or likely to happen. ◯

c Answer the questions.

1 What do you do if you feel tired during the day?
2 Which country would you go to if you could choose?
3 If you won a lot of money, what would be the first thing you would buy?
4 If you have some free time in the evening this week, what will you do?
5 If you could change one thing about yourself, what would it be?
6 How do you feel if you don't have breakfast in the morning?

d In groups, discuss your answers to exercise 3c.

Language assistant

Notice the order of the clauses and punctuation.
If I'm late, I'll call you.
I'll call you if I'm late.
Notice that *will* and *would* are rarely used in the *if* clause.

3 What if ...?

1 Speaking and listening

a Look at the scenes and try to guess what happened and what caused the problems.

b Listen to people talking about each incident and match the descriptions with the pictures.

    1 ....   2 ....   3 ....   4 ....

c Listen again to the people and answer the questions.

    1 What do you think feeling "under the weather" means?
    2 What was Jake's big mistake?
    3 Why was Cathy late leaving for the airport?
    4 What happened to Andrew's computer?
    5 What happened as a result?
    6 Why was it difficult for Jenny to get her car out?
    7 What's the worst thing for her?

d Listen again. Can you complete the missing final sentence in each incident? Listen and check your answers.

2 Grammar builder: unreal past conditionals

a Read these examples from the listening and answer the questions with *yes* or *no*.

1 *If I'd been more careful, I wouldn't have broken the mirror.*	Was I careful? Did I break the mirror?
2 *If I hadn't gone swimming, I wouldn't feel so ill now.*	Did I go swimming? Do I feel ill?

b Do you form these structures the same way in your language?

c Match the beginnings of the sentences with suitable endings.

1 I wouldn't feel so tired now if I ...
2 If I had bought that lottery ticket, I ...
3 She could have been a brilliant pianist if she ...
4 If they hadn't paid so much for that car, they ...
5 He might have won the match if he ...

a) had practiced more.
b) had gone to bed earlier.
c) had played more consistently.
d) would be wealthy now.
e) wouldn't be short of money.

3 Speaking and reading

a Look the picture. What do you think happened?

b Read the newspaper article quickly and put the paragraphs in the correct order.

1 .... 2 .... 3 .... 4 .... 5 ....

NEAR DISASTER ON JUMBO

A Hagan managed to overpower Mukonyi and co-pilot Richard Webb controlled and recovered the aircraft. The two pilots forced Mukonyi, 27, a Kenyan, into an upper-deck compartment, where he was handcuffed.

B Everything was apparently normal on the British Airways Boeing 747 flying from London to Kenya. The plane was flying over Sudan when a deranged passenger, Paul Kefa Mukonyi, suddenly burst into the cockpit and tried to take over the controls.

C Mukonyi is now being assessed by a Kenyan mental hospital. The pilots have suggested that he might have been spotted at check-in if more trained ground staff had been available to talk to passengers. Extra security measures already being suggested include passenger screening on all flights, locked flight deck doors and on-board security guards.

D The intruder struggled with Captain William Hagan and during the struggle, he managed to turn off the autopilot. The plane plummeted 10,000 feet, causing panic among the 379 passengers on board.

E After the struggle, 53-year-old Hagan, who was bitten on the ear, was later examined by doctors before leaving on vacation with his wife and two children. They were also on board during the incident.

> ### Learning tip
>
> You can use texts to teach yourself new words and phrases. In this text there is a useful group of words based on flying. You can also use texts to practice the strategy of guessing words from context. Work out the meaning of these words: *handcuffed* (paragraph A), *deranged* (B), *cockpit* (B), *passenger screening* (C), *plummeted* (D). In pairs, check your ideas. If necessary, check your answers in a dictionary.

c Underline all the words associated with flying in the text. Then organize them into groups. In pairs, discuss your categories and the meanings of any words you didn't know.

4 Writing, reading and speaking

a Work in groups of three. Imagine you were one of the people on the plane (e.g. the co-pilot, the captain's wife / child, one of the passengers). Each of you choose one person and write a short description of your experience on the flight.

b Read and compare your stories.

LANGUAGE for life:

career *management*

① Thinking about the future

What are your future career plans? Will you go to college? Will you go to vocational or technical school? Will you start work? Will you change jobs? How can you find out what is the best type of career for you? Once you've decided, how do you find more information about what the job involves and what prospects there are?

Read this career planning document for some ideas. Which ones appeal to you?

1 **Assess your strengths:** make a list of your strongest skills and abilities. Ask your family and friends for their input. Remember there are many kinds of intelligence. Are you good with words or figures? Are you skillful at building or fixing things? Maybe you have an artistic gift or a natural ability to help people.

2 **Gather career data:** try to find out information about different types of jobs, their pay, training and skill requirements, working conditions, schedules, advancement opportunities and projected growth.

3 **Tap into your network:** find out about the day-to-day realities of different occupations. Consider scheduling an "informational interview" with a professional in your field of interest. Discuss working conditions (alone/with others), the salary, training, promotion and the best and worst parts of the job.

4 **Research your labor market:** sometimes students will get a degree, only to discover their community is already saturated with qualified workers in their field. Check with companies or institutions in your field to see how many people they employ in your area, possible openings, and expected growth or decline.

5 **Take career tests:** many schools, universities and companies offer career guidance testing. Aptitude, interest and personality-style tests help you discover which careers would be most satisfying for you.

6 **Job shadow or volunteer:** get first-hand knowledge by seeing the job in action. Through job shadowing you can spend a day observing someone working in a job you're interested in. Or get actual work experience through voluntary work. Volunteering looks good on your résumé and is often a way into a job.

2 The right job

It's important to choose occupations that are likely to offer the best opportunities. Here are some factors you need to take into account.

Decide on the most important for you personally.

- *job satisfaction*
- *good pay and conditions*
- *ongoing training*
- *job security*
- *good working environment*
- *opportunities for promotion*

OK, so the job offers you things that are important for you, but are you the right person for the job? Qualifications are important, but so are personal qualities such as patience or an ability to make on-the-spot decisions.

What qualities do you think are needed for some of these jobs? And, most importantly, what qualities do you need for the careers that interest you?

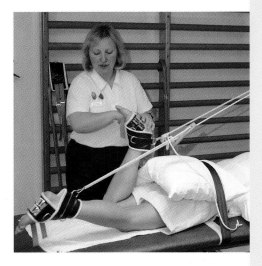

systems analysts	general managers and top executives
computer engineers	college professors physical therapists
marketing and advertising managers	commercial artists
instructors and coaches for sports and physical training social workers	

3 Your current situation

Now you've thought about your possibilities, it's time to make a career plan. A career plan identifies the most appropriate career direction for you and highlights the required skills and training. A career plan should help you make informed decisions on the action you should take next and will set out the steps for you to take to achieve your goals.

Complete the career plan and compare it with another student's. Now make a decision about what career you would most like to follow and think about short- and long-term goals of how you might achieve this.

4 Round-up

What have you decided about a future career? Discuss your ideas with a group of colleagues either using the information you've been looking at or your own ideas. Ask them to give you their advice and say whether they think you have made a good choice.

PLANNING STEPS	PERSONAL DATA
Your current career situation (school/college/job)	....
Your interests	....
Your values	....
Your skills	....
Your personality	....
Current labor market opportunities (where there are most jobs available	....
taking into account salaries, benefits, training)	....
Opportunities for your education, training and work experience	....
Your preferred options	....

Unit 10 Free time

1 Blood sports

1 Writing and reading

a What is the sport in the photograph? How much do you know about it?

b Write down any information you know about this sport. Then read the text quickly and add any new facts to your list.

ALL ABOUT BULLFIGHTING

Bullfighting has existed for 4,000 years. A form of this sport existed in ancient Crete. It was a popular spectacle in ancient Rome, but developed most in the Iberian Peninsula. Today the bullfight is more or less the same as it was in 1726 when the final details were introduced by Francisco Romero in Spain.

Every bullfight consists of a contest between six bulls and three matadors. The matadors, who kill the bulls, are the stars and can be paid as much as $25,000 per fight. Their distinctive costumes alone can cost several thousand dollars.

When the bull first comes into the arena, the matador does a series of passes with a large cape. Bulls frequently weigh more than 500 kilos so the danger is real. The second part of the spectacle consists of a *picador* on a horse sticking a lance into the bull's back. Following this *banderilleros*, working on foot, place *banderillas* (brightly adorned, barbed sticks) into the bull's shoulders to lower its head for the eventual kill.

At this stage, the bull is weaker and slower and the last phase of the fight begins. The matador uses a smaller cape to carry out a series of passes with the bull. This is the most dangerous part of the fight and most injuries occur here. Finally, the matador uses his sword to kill the bull by sticking the sword between the bull's shoulders.

Bullfighting is big business and is popular in Spain, Mexico, Peru, Venezuela, Colombia and Portugal. However, there is a lot of opposition to bullfighting from people who believe it is cruel and causes unnecessary suffering for the bulls.

c Write questions to match these answers about the text.

1 ....? For 4,000 years.
2 ....? Francisco Romero did.
3 ....? A contest between six bulls and three matadors.
4 ....? As much as $25,000 per fight.
5 ....? More than 500 kilos.
6 ....? They place barbed sticks into the bull's shoulders.
7 ....? By sticking a sword between the bull's shoulders.
8 ....? Because many people believe the sport is cruel.

2 Word builder: phrases giving opinion and (dis)agreeing

a   Look at the list of phrases and put them in the most suitable category.

> 1 I think …   2 You must be joking!   3 In my opinion …   4 I agree.   5 Absolutely!
>
> 6 If you ask me …   7 I disagree.   8 You're wrong!   9 You're right!   10 Do you really think so?
>
> 11 I'm not sure about that.   12 Nonsense!   13 Are you serious?   14 I don't think so.

Agree	Disagree	Giving an opinion	Strongly agree	Strongly disagree

b   It's important to use these phrases in the right context. For example, you wouldn't normally say "Nonsense!" to your boss! Decide if the phrases are formal / neutral (F/N) or informal (IN).

3 Listening and speaking

a   Listen to a conversation. How do the two people feel at the beginning and end of the conversation?

b   Listen to the conversation again and take notes of the arguments for and against bullfighting.

c   In groups, discuss who you agree with, Carol or Nicholas. Why? Give your arguments to your group. Try to use some of the expressions from exercise 2a.

4 Pronunciation: homophones

a   Homophones are words with the same pronunciation but different meanings and / or spellings. Look at these sentences. Which words are homophones?

The bulls are very weak at the end of the spectacle.

Every week thousands of people watch bullfights.

b   Look at the homophones. Listen and decide which word in each pair is used.

1 pair / pear   2 stair / stare   3 mail / male   4 peace / piece   5 heal / heel   6 sail / sale

5 Speaking and writing

a   Imagine bullfighting exists in your country. The Ministry of Culture is considering banning it. In groups, make a list of three reasons why you feel that it should or should not be banned.

b   In pairs, write a letter to the Minister of Culture stating why you think it is important to ban / not to ban the sport.

> Dear Sir / Madam,
>
> I am writing to you about the Government's proposal to ban bullfighting. I will outline the three main reasons why I strongly believe it should / should not be banned.
>
> In the first place, …
>
> Secondly, …
>
> Finally, …
>
> I hope that you will take these arguments into consideration when deciding on this issue.
>
> Yours faithfully,

2 A game of skill and luck

1 Speaking

In groups, look at these photographs of some of the most popular board games in the world. Can you name any of them? Do you know how they are played?

2 Writing and listening

a Have you ever played *Monopoly*? Do you know how to play it? What do you know about the origins of the game? You are going to listen to a talk about the game. Write three questions that you would like answered by the talk. Then listen and find out if they are answered.

b Listen to the talk again. Mark the statements T (true) or F (false).

1 Charles Darrow wasn't working when he invented *Monopoly*.   T ○   F ○
2 He produced the first version of the game in his office.   T ○   F ○
3 Parker Brothers was a successful department store.   T ○   F ○
4 The senior people in the company thought the game wasn't easy to play.   T ○   F ○
5 The company told Darrow the game could be a hit.   T ○   F ○
6 Darrow produced some games and sold them in a big store.   T ○   F ○
7 Parker Brothers realized the game was a success in Wanamaker's and decided to sell it.   T ○   F ○
8 The first-year sales of the game were disappointing.   T ○   F ○

c Work in small groups. Which board games are popular where you live? Do you like or dislike board games? Why?

3 Grammar builder: instructions

**Instructions can be expressed in different forms. Look at these instructions
from the rules of different games and write the numbers in the correct column.**

1   Players take turns to roll the dice.

2   If you have white pieces, put them on the white circles.

3   You have to roll a six to start the game.

4   Don't pick up more than three cards at a time.

5   You can't move the King more than one space in any direction.

6   Note there must be no empty spaces between your pieces.

7   You can't land on a square which already contains another player's pieces.

8   When you don't have the right card, you have to miss a turn.

What you should / must do in the game	What you shouldn't / mustn't do in the game

4 Reading and speaking

a   In pairs, read the instructions for the game *Hasami Shogi*.

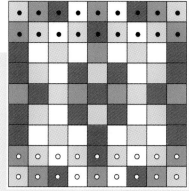

2 PLAYERS

To Start: Players pick black or white and choose 18
pieces. If you have black pieces, put them on the black
circles on the board. If you have white ones, put them
on the white circles. Decide who goes first.

Moving: Players take it in turns to move. A player can
move one or more spaces in any direction – forward,
backward, left, right – but not diagonally. All the spaces
passed over and that are landed on must be empty.

Jumping: Players can only jump over one other piece
when it is next to the jumper's starting spot. The
jumped-over piece can belong to either player, and it
cannot be removed afterwards. The jumper must land on
the space next to the jumped piece and that space must
be empty. The jumper has to stop there. Like moving,
jumping can go in any direction except diagonally.

Capturing:
Capturing is done
by making "capture
sandwiches." If a
player moves or
jumps so that their
piece is next to one
or more adjoining
enemy pieces, and if the player has another piece at the
other end of the line, the enemy piece(s) in between are
captured and removed from the board.

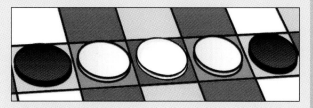

Winning: If a player has a chain of five connected pieces
of their color in a straight line, they are the winner. The
chain can be in any direction – vertical, horizontal or
diagonal. None of the pieces may be in the player's
original starting two rows.

b   When you feel confident you understand the rules, copy the board and play the game.

c   In groups, talk about what you liked and disliked about the game.

3 Let's get together

1 Listening and speaking

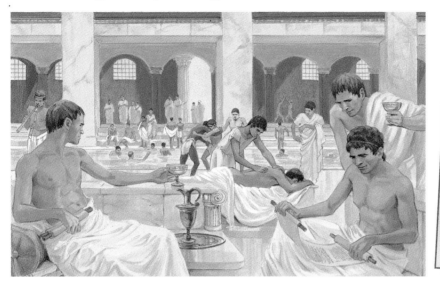

a Look at the pictures. Why do you think the Romans liked going to baths?

b Check (✔) the words you expect to hear in the talk. Then listen. Did you check the correct words?

sauna ⭕	gladiator ⭕	bathers ⭕ shampoo ⭕ fee ⭕ cool ⭕ exercise ⭕
store ⭕	religion ⭕	libraries ⭕ wine ⭕ snacks ⭕ forum ⭕ cleanest ⭕

c Work in pairs. Listen to the talk again and complete the fact table.

1	Features of ancient Roman baths	Running water, baths, flush toilets, ... and ....
2	Number of baths in Rome in the 4th century AD	Public .... Private ....
3	Date the bath of Diocletian was built	305 AD
4	Number of bathers the bath of Diocletian could accommodate	....
5	Different types of baths	Hot, ... and ....
6	Facilities	................, barbers, ..., restaurants and ....
7	Common activities in Roman baths	Bathe and talk, do ...., meet friends, do .... and get the latest news.
8	Times Romans went to the baths	Men .... Women ....

d Did anything surprise you about the Romans and their baths?

2 Grammar builder: review of adverbials

a Look at this short text, which contains eleven adverbs or adverbials. Find them and underline them. The first three have been done for you.

The <u>first time</u> I saw her was in the bar <u>downstairs</u>. She was singing in a band. She sang <u>extraordinarily</u> beautifully, but it wasn't her voice that attracted me to her. It was her eyes – green they were – green as the sea. She had nowhere to live so she moved into my place and we loved each other madly that long, cold winter. But as the time wore on we began to argue constantly. I often say to myself that we didn't always love well, but we did love truly.

> ### Language assistant
> Adverbials can be single words (adverbs), or phrases. Adverbs describe a verb, an adjective, another verb or a complete sentence. They tell us how often (frequency), when (time), how (manner), how much (degree) and where (place) something happens.
>
> *She **usually** sings **well**, but the **last time** I saw her she sang **beautifully** in the church.*

b Now classify the adverbs. Write them in the table.

Frequency	Time	Manner	Degree	Place
	first time		extraordinarily	downstairs

3 Speaking, reading and writing

a Look at the photograph in the article, but don't read yet. What does it tell you about the article?

b Work in groups. Write down some facts you know about coffee. Then read the article quickly to see how many of your facts appear.

THE COFFEE TRADITION

Coffee is one of the most popular drinks in the world and it has a long and varied history. The 9th century is the first recorded date when people drank coffee, in Arabia. Extensive planting of coffee first started in Yemen, in the Middle East, in the 15th century and it was forbidden to take coffee plants out of the country. However, plants were smuggled to India and Europe. In the late 16th century priests asked Pope Clement VIII to ban the evil drink of coffee but he refused! The first coffeehouse in London opened in the 1680s and soon there were coffeehouses all over the city. They were known as "penny universities" because you could buy a cup of coffee for a penny and learn more at the coffeehouse than in class!

In 1690, the Dutch introduced coffee cultivation to their colonies in Indonesia. Several decades later, coffee arrived in Latin America when the French brought a coffee plant to the island of Martinique. When a rare plant disease devastated the coffee plantations in south-east Asia in the mid-19th century, Brazil emerged as the world's foremost producer, which it still is today. The first espresso machine was made in France in 1822 and instant coffee was first marketed in 1909.

To give you an idea of the popularity of coffee, Starbucks Coffee opened in 1971 and today has 3,300 locations in ten countries. Why is coffee drinking so popular? People believe it has stimulating properties so it helps you concentrate or work. It also tastes good and everyone has their favorite type of coffee: cappuccino, espresso, iced, mocha.

c Group survey. Work in groups of four. Prepare a questionnaire: find out how many cups of coffee people drink a day, what type of coffee they prefer, when and why they drink coffee. If anyone doesn't drink coffee, find out why. Compare your results with another group.

LANGUAGE for life:

being *sociable*

① Questionnaire

Being able to socialize is an important quality for work, study and relaxing. However, a lot of people find socializing difficult. How sociable are you?

Answer the questionnaire and check your results to find out.

HOW SOCIABLE ARE YOU?

1 You see a group of people watching something. Your immediate reaction is to:
 a) observe with interest from a distance.
 b) walk the other way as quickly as possible.
 c) rush over and join the crowd.

2 You are at a party in a friend's house. Do you:
 a) talk to everyone with great enthusiasm?
 b) sit quietly sipping your drink, watching and feeling awkward?
 c) try to join in with the conversation when there's an opportunity?

3 You are on a bus for a two-hour journey. Do you:
 a) have a magazine ready but respond if someone tries to talk to you?
 b) break the ice with everyone and exchange life stories?
 c) read your book and try to sleep?

4 It's your first day at a new college. Without thinking too much, you:
 a) concentrate on the classes and keep a low profile.
 b) say "Hi!" to everyone and introduce yourself to as many people as possible.
 c) try to be friendly but check things out first.

5 You go to the office party but it's incredibly boring. Do you:
 a) organize dancing and party games with obligatory participation?
 b) wait for something to happen and avoid the people you dislike?
 c) wait for people to relax and then join in the fun?

6 You see someone you really like but hardly know walking towards you in the street. Do you:
 a) wait and see if she / he recognizes you and then react?
 b) take advantage of the opportunity to tell her / him all about yourself?
 c) look for a place to hide?

Scoring

1	a) 2	b) 1	c) 3
2	a) 3	b) 1	c) 2
3	a) 2	b) 3	c) 1
4	a) 1	b) 3	c) 2
5	a) 3	b) 1	c) 2
6	a) 2	b) 3	c) 1

Questionnaire key

14–18: You're super-sociable! You're the life and soul of any party. You're probably too busy socializing to read this!

9–13: You can be sociable when you want but you know how to be by yourself as well. You can get the best of both worlds.

0–8: You are one of the world's introverts. Shy and retiring, you are definitely not into being sociable.

② Analyze your personality

Now you've done the quiz, check out some more details about your kind of personality in this article. Then do a quick check with some people you know to see if this analysis is accurate.

ANALYZE YOUR PERSONALITY

Carl Jung, 1875-1961

Basic personality types of introvert and extrovert were first identified by Swiss psychoanalyst Carl Jung. In his view, introverts are shy, contemplative and reserved and tend to have difficulty adjusting to social situations. Extroverts, in contrast, are characterized by responsiveness to other people, activity, aggressiveness and the ability to make quick decisions. They also tend to be outgoing.

Modern psychologists have modified Jung's view. They have divided personality types into three basic groups: extroverts, introverts and ambiverts:

Extroverts are people oriented. They express emotions outwardly; they are inclined to put their ideas into action without a lot of thought about the results of those actions. Many extroverts choose careers as actors, salespeople, athletes and politicians.

Introverts contain their emotions rather than express them outwardly; they are concerned with cause and analysis of actions. They often prefer working alone to working with other people collectively. Introverts often choose careers in science, accounting, engineering, research and writing.

Ambiverts combine characteristics of extroverts and introverts. They usually adjust more easily to life's problems and are more successful in dealing with people. Ambiverts are often teachers or executives, and they make good parents.

③ Shyness and how to overcome it

If you have difficulty being sociable, it may be because you are shy. But don't despair, there are ways to deal with this.

Listen to Dr. Alexander Bannister talking about some ways to overcome shyness.

What do you think about his suggestions? Do you have any other suggestions of how to deal with shyness? Write them down and discuss them with other people in your group.

[5] Learning check

1 Progress check

a Choose the correct words for each sentence.

1 If Bill … here, he … know what to do. ………

    a) were / will   **b)** were / would   **c)** is / would

2 I usually … if I … to relax. ………

    a) exercise / want   **b)** will exercise / wanted   **c)** exercise / will want

3 If we … in a better climate, we … eat outside in the evenings. ………

    a) live / can   **b)** had lived / could   **c)** lived / could

4 We … the Jeep if we … enough money. ………

    a) would have bought / have   **b)** would buy / had had   **c)** would have bought / had had

5 The company worked … on the … project. ………

    a) quickly / special   **b)** quickly / specially   **c)** quick / special

b Complete the sentences with the correct form of the verb in parentheses.

6 Jack .... (be) delighted if you invite him to your wedding.

7 Karen wouldn't be here now if the police .... (not catch) the murderer.

8 When you .... (not know) the answer, you have to miss a turn.

9 We would have come in more quietly if we .... (know) the baby was asleep.

10 If you'd told me you needed more money, I .... (lend) you some.

c Read the sentences below. Check (✔) the correct sentences and correct the errors you find.

    I can't stay any longer. If I could, I ~~will~~.   ...*would*...

11 Paul is a very carefully driver.   ....

12 Sandra plays the piano very good.   ....

13 Mark always takes pictures wherever he goes.   ....

14 We prefer the bright colored paintings.   ....

15 I wouldn't have gone to the game if I didn't like soccer.   ....

2 Proficiency check

a Read the article and match these main ideas with the paragraphs. There are two main ideas for one of the paragraphs.

  a) By reading a sample, we can form an opinion about horoscopes.

    paragraph ………

  b) Horoscopes are effective because of the way they are written.   paragraph ………

  c) People have been interested in horoscopes for hundreds of years.   paragraph ………

  d) Horoscopes are very rarely specific in their predictions.   paragraph ………

A LOOK AT HOROSCOPES

1   For centuries many people have relied on the stars and planets to predict and explain events in their lives. Today, writing horoscopes is big business and they appear everywhere, in serious as well as not-
5   so-serious magazines and newspapers. Wherever there is a "human interest" section, there is probably a horoscope.

2   Can the planets really bring about changes in our
10   lives? And are the horoscopes that predict those changes accurate? Read this sample horoscope and judge for yourself: *This week could turn out to be an important one in your life. A big opportunity may be offered to you; if so, don't turn it down as it could*
15   *mean a change in your financial situation. And as for romance … If you're in a romance now, this should be a fabulous week for your relationship. If you're just getting over a broken heart, cheer up – a new romance may be on the horizon. And*
20   *remember, if you take time to be nice to people, they'll be nice to you.*

3   Horoscope writers are experts at two things. First, their predictions and advice tend to be general
25   enough so that they could prove true for almost anyone. And second, they usually stay away from words like *will, won't* and *definitely*. The predictions are expressed as possibilities, not facts.

b The following items are about inference: things that are implied by the writer but not directly said in the text. Choose the best completions for the sentences based on what the writer implies.

1   People who read horoscopes:
  a) usually have little education.
  b) are usually well-educated.
  c) come from many different educational backgrounds.

2   The horoscope in the text implies that:
  a) this will be a good week for you.
  b) this will be a bad week for you.
  c) you may have problems in relationships this week.

3   In the last paragraph, the author implies that:
  a) horoscopes don't really predict our future.
  b) people who write horoscopes aren't very good writers.
  c) horoscope writers are experts at predicting the future.

c Look at how the following multi-word verbs are used in the article. From the context, choose the correct meaning of each verb.

1   bring about (line 9)
  a) see   **b)** cause   **c)** show

2   turn out (line 12)
  a) finish   **b)** result   **c)** change

3   turn down (line 14)
  a) return   **b)** accept   **c)** refuse

4   get over (line 18)
  a) recover from   **b)** go away
  c) become ill with

5   cheer up (line 18)
  a) become happier   **b)** become sadder
  c) laugh

Unit 11 Furry friends

1 Preservation or extinction?

1 Word builder: similes

In pairs, try to complete the similes with the correct animals.

1 He's as strong as ... **a)** a mouse
2 She's as quiet as ... **b)** a fox
3 I'm as free as ... **c)** a mule
4 She's as smart as ... **d)** a turtle
5 He's as slow as ... **e)** an ox
6 You're as stubborn as ... **f)** a bird

> **Language assistant**
> One way of describing things or people is to use similes – phrases of comparison. In English, similes are formed with **as ... as**: *Before the storm, the sky was **as black as** night.* Many similes use animals as their point of comparison.

2 Pronunciation: weak forms and linking

a **In spoken English, words frequently become joined, or linked together and pronounced as one word. Look at this example and notice the linking.**

He's as slow as a turtle.

Listen to how the words are linked and to the pronunciation of *as* and *a*.

b **Practice saying the similes in exercise 1, linking the appropriate words. Then listen and compare your pronunciation with that on the cassette.**

c **Discuss whether any of the similes apply to people you know.**

My dad is as slow as a turtle. We always have to tell him to hurry up!

3 Reading

Read the article (opposite) about cloning and complete these statements.

1 The first paragraph is:
   a) an attack on cloning.   **b)** an argument in favor of cloning.   **c)** a general warning.
2 The second paragraph is ... cloning.
   a) an argument against   **b)** a factual account of   **c)** a fictional account of
3 The third paragraph is ... cloning.
   a) an argument for   **b)** a balanced view of   **c)** an argument against
4 In your opinion, is the author's general attitude toward cloning:
   a) positive?   **b)** negative?   **c)** neutral?

THE ETHICS OF PRESERVATION

We've all heard and used phrases like "hungry as a bear" or "smart as a fox." These phrases grew out of people's long association and familiarity with animals. But try to imagine a world where these were just abstract phrases because there were no more bears or foxes on earth. Many conservationists feel that if radical steps are not taken to preserve animal species and their habitats, that world could soon become reality.

Some scientists are experimenting with a controversial way to preserve endangered

species: cloning. In 1997, a sheep named Dolly became the world's first cloned mammal. In 2000, biologists cloned a gaur, an endangered species of Asian ox. To do this, they first collected skin cells from a gaur that had died. Then they retrieved eggs from normal cows which had been killed for meat. With a needle, they removed the nucleus from each egg and injected a gaur cell in its place. The eggs fused with the gaur cells and began to grow and

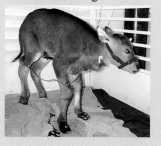

divide. These growing balls of cells were then implanted into mother cows. Only one of 44 implants survived and the result was Noah, a cloned gaur.

Naturally, there are strong arguments both in favor of and against cloning. The choices are not easy. Do we have the right to genetically engineer the future of certain species through cloning or other radical scientific procedures? On the other hand, do we have the right to stand by as more and more species become extinct? These are some of the difficult choices facing the generations of the 21st century.

4 Reading, writing and speaking

a Read the list of arguments about cloning. Mark each one F (for) or A (against).

1 Species should be allowed to evolve or disappear naturally. ....

2 Humans have an obligation to stop the destruction of species any way they can. ....

3 If species disappear, the balance of nature will be disrupted. ....

4 Not enough is known about the long-term effects of cloning. ....

5 It opens the door to unnatural creations like animals that are half pig and half cow! ....

6 Cloning can be controlled and limited to endangered animals. ....

b In pairs, try to add at least one more argument for and against cloning.

c In pairs, write a short paragraph for or against cloning. The phrases in the box may help you.

> **In our opinion, ...   Above all, ...   First, ...   Therefore, ...   Furthermore, ...   Finally, ...**

Cloning must be stopped. It is ...

Cloning is a fantastic scientific advance. With this, scientists will be able to ...

d Work with a pair of students who have the opposite opinion from yours. Use the arguments in your paragraph and any other arguments you can think of to try to change their opinion.

97

2 Responsible ownership

1 Reading and speaking

a Read the first part of an animal protection society brochure. In each of the two cases, what were the crimes against the animal? Were they crimes of negligence or of cruelty?

Consider the following scenarios. Read them and take a moment to really think about them.

A family gives their child an adorable puppy for Christmas. By June, he is eight months old and not so cute anymore. In fact, he's impossible. They hit him constantly to punish him for bad behavior, but he doesn't change. The child has lost interest and they can't find a new home for the dog. One day, they put him in the car, drive out to a country road, put him out of the car and drive away. The young dog is terrified and confused. He runs after the car until it disappears and he falls down, exhausted and afraid, abandoned by the people he has loved and trusted.

Another family has a cat, a member of the family for ten years. The family decides to go away for a week and they leave the cat alone. They leave plenty of food and water, but it's wintertime in New York and they turn off the heat. Not used to extreme cold, the old cat catches a respiratory infection. His lungs fill with fluid and he can't breathe. Alone, and without veterinary attention, he dies.

b Before you read the rest of the brochure, discuss what points people should consider before they decide to get a pet.

c Now read the rest of the brochure. Were there any points mentioned that you didn't think of? Did you think of any points that weren't mentioned?

The cases above are only two examples of the endless cases of cruelty and neglect inflicted on animals by humans. If you plan to take an animal into your house, <u>please</u> consider the following questions.

1   Are all the members of your household in agreement about getting a pet?

2   Do you have the financial ability to pay for adequate food, worm treatments and vaccinations, and the occasional medical emergency?

3   Do you have enough time, and enough patience, to train the animal, play with it and take care of its needs?

4   If the animal is for a child, are you willing to accept most of the responsibility for caring for it? Children may have good intentions, but they are usually inconsistent with pet care!

5   Will you be responsible about birth control? Many people like the fun of having puppies or kittens, but remember, it's difficult to find good homes for them!

6   Are you prepared to care for the animal all its life? It isn't easy to find homes for unwanted animals!

Think carefully about these questions, and answer them honestly. If you realize that "no" is the answer to any of them, then please reconsider your plan to get a pet. There are far too many poorly cared for, unhappy or abandoned animals in the world.

d **Which title do you think is most appropriate for the article? Why?**

1 A case of cruelty
2 Questions for pet owners
3 A pet is not just for Christmas

2 Listening and speaking

a Jennifer has just gotten a new puppy and Sally is thinking about getting one. Listen to their conversation. Do you think either of them will have problems as a dog owner? Why?

b Now listen to their conversation two months later. Answer the questions.

1 What are the problems with the puppy?
2 What is the owner doing wrong?
3 What does her friend recommend?
4 Is she going to take her friend's advice?

3 Speaking

In groups, discuss good and bad treatment of animals you have seen. What can you do if you know of an animal that is being neglected or mistreated?

4 Grammar builder: review of *hope* and *wish*

a Look at these sentences. Which ones refer to present or past situations or actions that the speaker wants to change, but which cannot be changed? Which refer to situations or actions that the speaker would like to happen?

1 I hope my boyfriend will help me!
2 I wish I hadn't gotten a dog!
3 I wish I knew what to do.
4 I wish I didn't have to give him away.
5 I hope I can find a good home for him.

b Use *wish* or *hope* to comment on the following situations.

1 something you want to have happened, but you aren't sure it did happen
I hope my boyfriend bought tickets for the dog show.
2 a mistake you made in the past
3 something in your life which you would like to change but can't
4 something you want to happen in the future
5 something you would like to be able to do but can't

Language assistant:
hope and *wish*

Hope: is used with a variety of tenses.
*I hope you **like** my present. / I hope Sally **will help** me.* = present hope, future action
*I hope you're **enjoying** your vacation.* = present hope, present action.
*I hope Bill **has called** the vet. / I hope Kathy **got** the job.* = present hope, past action.

Wish: for present wishes we use the past simple: *I wish I **had** a job.*
For present or future wishes we use *would* (about other people) or *could*: *I wish Mark **would train** his dog. / I wish I **could speak** Japanese.*
For past regrets we use the past perfect: *I wish I **hadn't gotten** this dog.*

3 Animals as healers and teachers

1 Speaking, reading and writing

a In groups, discuss the benefits of having a pet.

b Read the article quickly and match the topics with the paragraphs.

Paragraph 1   **a)** animal educators

Paragraph 2   **b)** how to get involved

Paragraph 3   **c)** how animals benefit human health

Paragraph 4   **d)** help for an emotionally disturbed child

A dog is a man's best friend.

There's something about the outside of a horse that's good for the inside of a man.

ANIMAL HELPERS

1   In today's world of high-tech science and medicine, a very low-tech healer has been discovered – animal companionship. It is now well documented that people with certain problems like heart disease or cancer live longer and have a better recovery rate if they have pets. Contact with pets lowers blood pressure and reduces stress. Animals are increasingly important in therapy for people with Alzheimer's disease, autism and cerebral palsy. These people frequently suffer from frustration and depression, as well as physical problems. Activities with animals help them with physical coordination and also give them joy, entertainment and loving companionship.

2   Here is a case which illustrates the therapeutic qualities of animals. Brandon was a six-year-old elective mute: he simply didn't want to talk. His older cousin had a nice dog and he began taking it to see Brandon. He didn't try to force Brandon to speak, but he let him pet the dog, and he demonstrated simple commands like "Sit" and "Come." One day Brandon suddenly said "Come!" and when the dog went to him, he laughed and said "Good dog." If Brandon hadn't had contact with that dog, he might not be speaking today.

3   Another growing use for animal companions is in schools. In some cases, animals are used to help children with physical or emotional problems. In others, they are used for sharing and socialization activities, or simply to teach children about animals.

4   If you would like to know more about animal therapy and companion programs, you can contact The American Humane Society or do a search under animal therapy on the Internet. You don't have to be an animal trainer or a therapist to get involved, especially in animal companion programs in schools, hospitals or homes for the elderly.

c Read the article again. Summarize the main ideas of paragraphs 2–4 in one or two sentences.

Paragraph 1: *Animal therapy is useful in helping people with both physical and emotional problems.*

2 Grammar builder: mixed conditionals

a It is often possible to mix the tenses in conditional sentences, i.e. to use tense combinations other than the traditional conditional types.

If you'll take a seat, I can find out when he'll be ready.

If he really loved you, he wouldn't have said that.

Look at the underlined verbs in these sentences and identify the tenses.

1	If all that you said <u>is</u> true, we<u>'ve made</u> a mistake.	E / D -R
2	If I <u>were</u> you, I <u>wouldn't have said</u> that.	....
3	If everyone <u>has arrived</u>, we<u>'ll leave</u> in five minutes.	....
4	If Sam <u>is</u> in New York, he <u>didn't go</u> to the conference in Boston.	....
5	If we <u>had told</u> Jim about the meeting, he <u>would</u> be here.	....
6	We<u>'ll bring</u> some food if you<u>'ll provide</u> all the drinks.	....

A future simple
B past perfect
C past simple
D present perfect
E present simple
F *would*
G *would* + present perfect

b Are the conditionals in these sentences real (possible) or unreal (impossible)? Write R or U. Then find an example of one real and one unreal conditional in the article in exercise 1. To what time periods do the clauses refer?

c Complete the sentences with the correct verb forms.

1 If Marsha hasn't arrived yet, she probably .... (come) at all.

2 If Bob was at the party last night, I .... (not see) him.

3 If you had asked her to marry you, she .... (be) by your side now!

4 I still wouldn't know about their problems if you .... (not tell) me.

5 If you can't figure out the answer, then we .... (not give) you enough information.

6 I .... (call) Joe to tell him about the meeting if you'll call Sandra.

3 Listening

a A group of friends want to become involved in animal companion activities. Listen to their discussion. What type of activity do they decide on?

b Listen again and answer these questions.

1 What three groups of people do they think about working with?

2 What are the problems with the first two types?

3 What type of animals is the group going to work with?

4 What three topics are they going to offer?

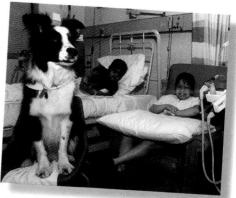

4 Speaking

In groups, discuss the following.

1 Talk about any cases you know of where animals have helped people with physical or emotional problems.

2 If you were going to choose one area in this field to work in, which would you choose and why?

3 Discuss ways in which pet owners could help people in your community.

LANGUAGE for life:
traveling with *Rover*

① A traveler's tale

This is the first part of a story told to *Dog World* by a young traveler. How do you think it ends?

PART ONE

It was snowing on the mountain and I was lost. Without food or shelter my chances for survival were close to zero; still, I struggled on, cold and exhausted. Suddenly, I heard the sound of low growling. Through the snow I could see the glare of yellow eyes – I was surrounded by wolves! To them, I represented a welcome meal after weeks in the Alaskan winter with almost no food. I ran futilely for a few steps, then the wolves were on me. My eyes were closed in fear, but I could feel the weight of one of the great beasts on my chest and its breath in my face ...

And now for the second part of the story. Did you guess the ending?

PART TWO

I opened my eyes and saw a great hairy face, its nose an inch from my face. They will kill me now, I thought. And then, to my great relief, I realized that it wasn't a wolf at all, but my German shepherd, Sniffer. We were camping in Colorado (not Alaska) and I had been dreaming. I was cold because Sniffer had pulled all the covers off me. The weight I had felt on my chest was the dog stretched out full-length on top of me and the growling was Sniffer snoring. He, at least, wasn't suffering from bad dreams! Sometimes traveling with a dog can be a nightmare!

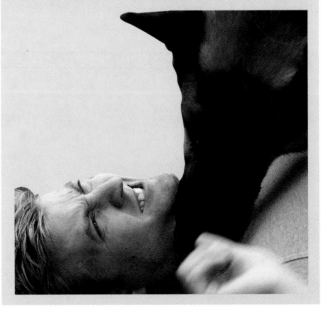

Preparing for a trip

Imagine that you are going to the U.S. for a month. You want to take your dog. Are you prepared? Take this quiz to find out.

1 Airlines will not take animals if the weather is very hot or cold. T ○ F ○

2 Animals must be tranquilized before flying. T ○ F ○

3 You must observe regulations about the size of animal shipping cages. T ○ F ○

4 Pets must have special animal "passports." T ○ F ○

5 Leashes are required for dogs in most parks, beaches and public areas. T ○ F ○

6 If your animal becomes ill in the U.S., you can buy most veterinary medicines without a prescription. T ○ F ○

Now check your answers. Are you a pet-smart traveller?

CHECK YOUR ANSWERS. ARE YOU A PET-SMART TRAVELER?

1 True. Especially if the animal has to be transferred from one flight to another, airlines won't ship it in extreme weather. Animals may be outside while waiting for a transfer and they could die from extreme heat or cold.

2 False. Tranquilize the animal only if it seems extremely nervous on the day of travel. Follow your vet's instructions exactly.

3 True. The animal must be able to stand up in the cage.

4 False. Only vaccination certificates are required. Check with the local embassy or consulate, or with your vet.

5 True. Leashes are required in almost all public areas, including beaches and national parks.

6 False. Most veterinary medicines, like human medicines, require a prescription.

Animals across cultures

Different countries and cultures have different attitudes about animal tourists.

In France, pets are frequently allowed in restaurants. Sometimes waiters will even ask what the animal would like to eat! Do not try this in Britain or the U.S.

Of course, these are generalizations. As with any generalization, there are infinite numbers of variations!

In your experience, what is the situation in your country?

● *Are animals allowed to travel freely from one area of the country to another?*
● *Do dogs have to be kept on a leash in public places?*
● *Are animals allowed in hotels? In restaurants? In campsites?*
● *Are people generally afraid of dogs or friendly to them?*

Learning from experience

Have you, or has anyone you know, ever traveled with an animal? What were the positive aspects of the experience? Were there any problems? What would you recommend for future trips with animals?

Unit 12 Using language skills

1 Read to learn

1 Recognizing genre

a   This skill is about the ability to identify features which are characteristic of different texts, e.g. a comic, an advertisement, an autobiography, an academic article. Scan the three excerpts below. Which one is from a novel? A biography? A newspaper editorial?

A

When Jim Hanson attended high school in the 1970s, few young people in his inner city neighborhood aspired to higher education. Many didn't even finish high school, as financial pressures
5   caused them to start working at an early age. However, Jim's high school, recognizing its students' need for technical skills, had a strong vocational program which included courses in building construction. Jim took courses in carpentry,
10 computer drafting and design, often staying after school to work on his projects. His grades in all subjects were good and in his vocational courses they were outstanding. In 1975, his senior year, the hard work paid off in the form of a full scholarship
15 to study architecture at New York University.

B

If Jim Hanson is allowed to build Barton Creek Mall, he will be contributing to the destruction of species and the pollution of Barton Creek. One of our last local
5   wilderness areas will disappear. Furthermore, Hanson and his supporters say that they have the interests of the people in mind. If that is true, then why are they offering less than market value
10 to the farmers who own the land where the mall will be built? Hanson Construction is taking advantage of people's economic necessity to cheat them out of a fair price. The only interest
15 Jim Hanson has in mind is his own.

C

Sally stayed after the meeting to talk to some of the other organizers of the protest against the construction of the new shopping mall in the Barton Creek Wilderness Area. When she left, it
5   was after 10:00 p.m., and as she crossed the parking lot to her car she felt uneasy, almost frightened. Arriving at her car, she saw that her fears had been justified. Her tires were slashed and in red paint scrawled across the car door was the
10 message: YOU'RE NEXT.

The young police officer who took the report was sympathetic but gave Sally little hope that the people who had damaged her car would be found. "I'm very sorry about your car," he said. "I'm afraid
15 you've been the victim of a vicious practical joke by some high school kids." But Sally didn't think it was a joke. As the leader of the movement to stop the construction before the Barton Creek area was destroyed, she had met Jim Hanson, and she had
20 seen the hard look in his eyes as he vowed not to let anything stop his Barton Creek project.

b Talk about how you decided on the genre for each text. Consider characteristics such as the following.

- formal / informal tone
- formal / informal vocabulary
- subjective opinions / facts
- dialog / monolog

2 Making inferences

a This skill is "reading between the lines" or understanding ideas which are not specifically stated in words. Mark the sentences T (true) or F (false).

1 It was unusual that Jim Hanson went to college.   T ◯ F ◯
2 He probably came from a poor family.   T ◯ F ◯
3 The editor is in favor of the Barton Creek project.   T ◯ F ◯
4 In the editor's opinion at least, Jim Hanson is a rich man. T ◯ F ◯
5 Sally suspected that she might have problems with the
   construction company.   T ◯ F ◯
6 She believed that the damage to her car was a practical joke. T ◯ F ◯

b In groups, discuss how you decided on the answers.

3 Working out meaning from context

a This skill is about the ability to use clues in a text to discover the meaning of words and phrases that you did not know before. Match the words on the left with the meanings on the right. Look back at the contexts of the words in the texts in exercise 1a.

1 outstanding (text A, line 13)   a) promised
2 paid off (text A, line 14)   b) written
3 cheat (text B, line 13)   c) trick
4 fair (text B, line 14)   d) was worth the trouble
5 uneasy (text C, line 6)   e) excellent
6 slashed (text C, line 8)   f) cut
7 scrawled (text C, line 9)   g) nervous
8 vowed (text C, line 20)   h) just

b In pairs, compare your answers. Discuss how the contexts helped you to understand the meanings of the words.

4 Write your own Learning tip

a In pairs, complete the Learning tip with your own ideas.

b Share your Learning tip with your classmates. Discuss the different ideas and add to your Learning tip if you want to.

Learning tip

Reading in English can help you to ...
When you don't know a word, first try to ...
It's a good idea to read ...

2 Writing in the right tone

1 Tone of voice in letters

Below are two business letters. Read them and decide which one is more appropriate in a business situation. Underline the phrases or sentences that make the more formal letter more appropriate.

A

CENTRAL CEMENT AND CONCRETE

Mr. George Lincoln
Accounts Manager
Barker Construction Company

April 30, 2001

Dear Mr. Lincoln,

I am writing in reference to 25,000 bags of cement ordered from our Cedar Park branch on April 8, invoiced on April 15.

I believe you are aware that our company policy states that invoices be paid within ten days of receipt. When your payment was not received by April 25, we assumed there had been a clerical error and my assistant called your accounting department to check. I am afraid they were not very co-operative and told her that the payment would not be made this month.

If it would be helpful, I would be happy to speak to you personally about the payment. I would be grateful if we could reach an agreement as soon as possible and hope that we can continue to have an excellent working relationship.

Sincerely,

Bruce Thomas
Accounts Manager

B

CENTRAL CEMENT AND CONCRETE

Mr. George Lincoln
Accounts Manager
Barker Construction Company

April 30, 2001

Dear Mr. Lincoln,

How are you doing? I'm writing about 25,000 bags of cement ordered from our Cedar Park branch on April 8, invoiced on April 15.

As you know, our company requires payment within ten days of receipt of an invoice. When we didn't get your payment by April 25, my assistant called your accounting department to check. They were pretty rude and told her that the payment would not be made this month.

Please call me because I want to speak to you personally about the whole thing. We need to reach an agreement as soon as possible.

All the best,

Bruce Thomas
Accounts Manager

Language assistant

Grammar can help to indicate levels of formality. Notice which modals are used in the formal sentences.

Formal: **Would** you mind if I used your computer for a little while?

I **would** very much appreciate it if you **could** call me a few days before the meeting.

It **might** be better if you didn't tell Laura about our conversation.

Informal: Can you please bring me some water?

Call me and let me know what time we need to leave.

Don't wait until the last minute to pay your bills!

2 Writing a letter

a In pairs or small groups, follow the steps below to write a formal letter.

1 Read the situation below and brainstorm the points you want to make.
2 Decide how you want to divide the main points into paragraphs.
3 Write a first draft and check it together. Consider what grammar and vocabulary can give your letter the correct level of formality. Look back at the formal letter in exercise 1 for ideas.
4 Write the final draft.

Situation:

You are the contractor in charge of building a new bank. You have ordered bricks for the construction from the Madison Brick and Stone Company. You pre-paid the order and the bricks were supposed to be delivered a week ago. You can't continue construction without them and every day of delay costs an extra $1,000. You have called the warehouse manager, but he won't guarantee a delivery date. In groups, write a letter to the director of the company explaining the problem.

b Put your letters on the wall. Read them and discuss the language used. Are some more formal than others? Do they explain the problem clearly? Do they demand a solution without being rude? Ask your teacher about any parts of your letter you had difficulty with.

3 Write your own Learning tip

a In pairs, complete the ideas for a Learning tip about writing.

b Share your Learning tip with your classmates. Discuss the different ideas and add to your Learning tip if you want to.

Learning tip

Before you start writing a letter, think about ...
When you write a business letter, the language should be ...
Before you send the letter, it's a good idea to ...

3 The art of listening

1 Listening strategies and subskills

a When we listen, we use certain strategies to help our comprehension, especially in a foreign language. These strategies include, among other things:

- asking for repetition
- asking for clarification
- checking understanding of details
- summarizing the main points

Discuss what you would do in the following situations.

1 The person you are talking to speaks very fast and uses a lot of slang.

2 The conversation is very technical and there are several important words you don't understand.

3 You are at a workshop at a conference and you haven't completely understood one of the main points.

4 A person gives you a set of fairly long and complicated instructions.

5 A person has given you a rather long explanation of something and you want to make sure you've understood the main ideas.

6 Someone has given you instructions about the time and place of an important meeting. You want to make sure you have all the information.

b We listen for different reasons in different situations. Match these situations with the reasons for listening below.

1 You're sitting in on a lecture to find out if you might be interested in taking the course. ....

2 You're on the telephone and someone gives you their address and telephone number. ....

3 You're listening to some English songs in your room. ....

4 You want to understand if a friend is happy with something you have suggested. ....

a) You want to make sure you have all the correct details.

b) You are listening for pleasure and to try to understand a little.

c) You only want to understand the general idea, not the details.

d) You want to listen "between the lines", i.e. understand the feelings as well as the words.

2 Listening for the general idea

You are going to hear two short conversations. For each one, choose the sentence which summarizes the topic or main idea of the conversation.

Conversation 1

1 What are the man and woman discussing?

a) A sports game.   b) A professor's competence.

c) An exam.

Conversation 2

2   What is the couple's opinion of the restaurant?

   a) They don't like it.   **b)** They like it very much.   **c)** The man likes it but the woman doesn't.

🎧 3 Listening for detail

For these two short conversations, there are two questions about details. Read the questions first. Then listen and choose the correct answer.

Conversation 1

1   Where does the woman want to go?

   a) To a party.   **b)** To work.   **c)** To the library.

2   Why does John say he might not want to go?

   a) He has to work late.   **b)** He has to study.   **c)** He's tired.

Conversation 2

3   Why does the woman want to cancel the meeting?

   a) She has an appointment.   **b)** Her son is going to the doctor.

   c) She has to make an important phone call.

4   What is the man going to do?

   a) Go to the meeting.   **b)** Reschedule the meeting.   **c)** Say that the woman will call.

🎧 4 Listening for inference

In these two short conversations, the questions are about inference – what the people *imply* with words or tone of voice. Listen and choose the correct answers.

Conversation 1

1   What does the woman imply?

   a) She wants to go out.   **b)** She doesn't want to go out.

   c) She doesn't like Bob and Sally.

2   What does the man imply?

   a) The woman is tense.   **b)** She's relaxed.   **c)** She doesn't feel well.

Conversation 2

3   What did the man think of the exam?

   a) It was easy.   **b)** It was difficult.   **c)** He didn't take it.

4   What does the woman think of John's comment about his grade?

   a) She's sure he got an A.   **b)** She doesn't believe he got an A.   **c)** She's sure he failed.

5 Write your own Learning tip

a   In pairs, complete the Learning tip on listening with your own ideas.

b   Share your Learning tip with your classmates. Discuss the different ideas and add to your Learning tip if you want to.

> **Learning tip**
>
> When you listen to a long conversation or lecture, try to focus on ...
> When you are listening, don't worry about ...
> When you are talking to someone, it is helpful to notice ...

4 Say what you mean

The activities in the lesson have been designed to let you see how fluent you've become, so don't worry too much about perfect grammar. Just open your mouth and communicate!

1 Charades

Play in groups or as a class.

- The teacher gives one student a word.
- The student mimes the word silently and his / her classmates try to guess what it is.
- After playing the game for a few minutes with words, change to sentences!
- The student who guesses the word or sentence does the next mime.

2 Explain this!

Work in groups of four or five. You will have to explain why you were at a certain place or doing a particular thing at a particular time.

- One student chooses a classmate in the group and reads one of the situations below.
- The classmate has to give a logical explanation for why he / she was in that situation.
- This student then chooses another classmate and another situation.
- When each student has given an explanation, vote on the most logical explanation and also the most creative explanation.

1 You were in the middle of a fountain in the park with clothes and shoes on last Saturday afternoon.

4 You were climbing in the window of your neighbor's house last night.

2 You were coming out of the Ritz Hotel with a group of your friends at about 11:00 p.m. last night, laughing.

5 You were running on the beach wearing only a towel last Saturday morning.

3 You were being driven across town in the back of a police car on Friday night.

6 You were sitting in a tree in the park in the middle of a storm yesterday afternoon.

3 Chain story

Work in groups of six to eight. You are going to invent a story.

- One student is the time keeper, and another student starts the story.
- Each student must talk for thirty seconds. After each thirty seconds the time keeper says *Stop* and the next student in the circle continues the story.
- Start like this: *An amazing thing happened to me yesterday ...*

4 Educated guesses

a **Work with a classmate you think you know quite well. Without consulting with your partner, complete the statements below the way you think he / she would complete them. Then complete them for yourself.**

	Your partner	You
1 My favorite time of day is ...		
2 On weekends I love to ...		
3 My favorite kind of food is ...		
4 I usually spend my vacations in ...		
5 I don't like people who ...		
6 I think politicians should ...		
7 I've never ...		
8 If I won the lottery, I would ...		
9 I'd like to learn to ...		
10 When I finish this English course, I'm going to ...		

b **With another pair of students, check how many statements you and your partner completed correctly for each other. The pair with the most matches wins.**

5 Write your own Learning tip

a **In pairs, write a Learning tip about the future of your English – ideas for maintaining or improving the English you have learned.**

b **Share your ideas in groups or with your class. Discuss your plans for using your English in the future.**

6 Learning check

Proficiency check: using English in real life

a Understanding public notices

You are in an American airport. What does each sign below mean?
Choose the best explanation (a–d).

1
> **DOMESTIC DEPARTURES TO THE LEFT** ◀|||

a) Go to the left if you wish to leave the airport.
b) Turn left for flights back home to your country.
c) You must leave your personal possessions here.
d) Go left if you are taking a flight within this country.

....

2
> **HOLDERS OF NON-U.S. PASSPORTS THIS WAY** |||▶

a) Do not present non-American passports here.
b) American citizens should go this way.
c) If you do not have a U.S. passport, go through here.
d) You can get an American passport here.

....

3
> **DO NOT LEAVE BAGGAGE UNATTENDED**

a) Remember to take your bags with you when you leave.
b) Stay with your suitcases and keep an eye on them.
c) Pay attention to your bags when you leave.
d) Get an attendant to help you with your bags.

....

b Finding information

You are in Chicago and want information about the things below (1-3). Which booklet on the right (A-E) will give you the best information about each topic? Write the letter of the correct booklet beside the information.

1 Cheap but satisfactory and fairly central places to stay. ....
2 What to see and do as a visitor in the city. ....
3 Where to meet people of your age in a healthy environment. ....

A
THE NIGHT IS YOUNG
If you are too, and you want to have good clean fun with others like you, this is the guide you're looking for.

B
TOP CHICAGO HOTELS
More than 20 hotels that you'll really love to be in, all up to the very high standard you're used to and deserve.

C
THE REAL CHICAGO
This short history tells you much you didn't know about Chicago before, during and after the brief age of Al Capone.

D
CHICAGO MUSTS
Everything you must not miss while in Chicago and a lot of extra options too. Know the best of our great city.

E
BARGAIN ACCOMMODATIONS
A great selection of good downtown hostels, boarding houses, etc. Ideal for students and budget travelers.

c Being clear and correct

You are writing to thank someone who was kind to you in Chicago. Choose the most appropriate words or phrases from the box to complete the paragraph of the letter. There are two words or phrases too many.

hope	would not have	want
did not have	expect	had not	wish

d Giving information in writing

You are suddenly going to Chicago again – a trip to a conference paid for by your college / company. Write and tell your friend. Use the information in the travel agent's note.

If you (1) .... been so kind to me, I (2) .... such wonderful memories of Chicago now. I really (3) .... I had been able to stay longer, but I know I'll be back some day. I (4) .... you can come to stay with me here in the summer as we planned. But I (5) .... you will find my little city boring compared with Chicago.

Dear Deborah,
I have a surprise for you – (1) .... to Chicago in two weeks! Isn't that great? The reason is that (2) ....
   I'm flying on (3) ...., American Airlines flight no. (4) .... It arrives (5) .... Don't worry about meeting me; I'll take an airport bus into the city.
   I'm staying for (6) .... and I'm leaving on (7) ...., American Airlines again. It departs (8) .... I really hope that we can (9) .... while (10) ....
Yours,

MARCO POLO TOURS

Dep.	07:45 (June 16) AA645 (American Airlines)
Arr.	Chicago 14:25

Dep.	Chicago 10:20 (June 30) AA640
Arr.	18:10

e Getting the message

You get home from work and find a message on your answering machine. It's from your friend in Chicago. She has some important information for you. Listen to the message and complete the notes.

Deborah – in Chicago from .... to ....

Key to her apartment with .... in apt. ....

Plan for weekend of .... to go to ....

Songsheet 1
Englishman in New York

1 Reading and speaking

In pairs, take this quiz with a partner and find out who knows the most about Sting, the singer of this song.

1 Which rock group did Sting use to play with?

a) The Police　　　b) Queen　　　c) UB40

2 Which instrument did he play in the group?

a) lead guitar　　　b) bass guitar　　　c) drums

3 What was his job before he became a musician?

a) teacher　　　b) pilot　　　c) builder

4 What is his real name?

a) Andy Summers　　　b) Stuart Copeland　　　c) Gordon Sumner

5 Which animal does his nickname "Sting" come from?

a) bee　　　b) bird　　　c) bull

6 Which English city does he come from?

a) London　　　b) Bristol　　　c) Newcastle

7 Which Sting song is the basis for Puff Daddy's huge hit *I'll be missing you*?

a) *Roxanne*　　　b) *Every breath you take*　　c) *Message in a bottle*

8 Complete the titles of these songs by Sting.

a) They dance *alone / together / every day*

b) *Fresh / Another / Brand* new day

c) Desert *song / rose / storm*

9 Which charity was Sting involved in setting up in 1989?

a) Band Aid　　　b) Oxfam　　　c) The Rainforest Foundation

10 How many children does Sting have?

a) 4　　　b) 6　　　c) 3

2 Listening

a *Englishman in New York* was inspired by a real person, Quentin Crisp, an elderly Englishman who moved to New York. Listen to the song and complete the notes.

1 He drinks ....

2 He always carries ....

3 If people treat him with ignorance, he ....

4 He thinks it's important to be ....

5 Because he's a gentleman, he never ....

b Now look at the song and check your answers. Then try to guess some of the missing words before you listen again.

Englishman in New York

I don't drink coffee, I take tea my dear
I like my (1) .... done on the side
And you can hear it in my (2) .... when I talk
I'm an Englishman in New York

See me walking down (3) ....
A walking cane here at my side
I take it (4) .... I walk
I'm an Englishman in New York

Chorus
I'm an alien; I'm a legal alien
I'm an Englishman in New York
I'm an alien; I'm a legal alien
I'm an Englishman in New York

If "manners maketh man" as someone said
Then he's the (5) .... of the day
It takes a man to suffer ignorance and smile
Be yourself, no (6) .... what they say

Repeat chorus

Modesty, propriety can lead to notoriety
You could end up as the (7) ....
Gentleness, sobriety are rare in this society
At night a (8) .... 's brighter than the sun

Takes more than combat gear to make a man
Takes more than (9) .... for a gun
Confront your enemies, (10) .... them when you can
A gentleman will walk but never run

3 Word builder: synonyms

Find words or expressions from the song with the same meaning as those below.

1 a foreigner
2 the opposite of pride
3 correct behavior in public
4 fame for doing something wrong
5 seriousness
6 a soldier's uniform

4 Speaking

"Manners maketh man" is a famous quotation. *Maketh* is the old form of *makes*. It means that manners (the way you behave in society) are extremely important. In groups, discuss the questions.

1 What examples of good manners can you find in the song?
2 What do you think Sting especially admired about this person?
3 Tell your partners about a person you know who lives life differently from the people around him / her.
4 Which of these things do you think you would change if you went to live in New York?

- the food you eat
- the clothes you wear
- the way you travel
- your hobbies
- your daily routine
- your manners

Songsheet 2
Private emotion

1 Reading and speaking

Read this brief biography of the singer Ricky Martin and find seven more factual mistakes. Compare your answers with your partner.

R icky Martin was born in Hata Rey, ~~Mexico~~ *Puerto Rico* on Christmas Eve 1971. His full name is Enrique Martin Morales IV and he has five brothers and sisters. He began acting at the age of six and tried to join the famous teen group Take That several times, but was rejected because he couldn't dance. He finally joined at the age of 12 and enjoyed five years of success, before leaving to complete his schooling.

After this, he launched a solo career, which he combined with acting, first in Mexico and then in the United States. In the U.S. he first became famous for his role as Miguel in the long-running series *Friends*. He also achieved great success on the Broadway stage for his role in the musical *Les Misérables*, based on the play by Shakespeare. Apart from these main roles, he made a number of commercials and even provided the voice for the Disney character Tarzan, in the Spanish version of the movie.

But by the late 1990s, he no longer had the time for his acting. His song, *La copa de la vida*, recorded for the 1998 Olympics in France, became a huge hit in Europe. He spent the following year touring the world, as his album, *Ricky Martin*, sold millions. It seemed that everyone wanted to work with him – even Michael Jackson sang with him on the song *Be Careful* – and, of course, the fact that he is fluent in five languages helped him to communicate with fans all over the world.

2 Listening

a   Before you listen, use the pictures to guess what the missing words are.

b   Now listen to the song and check your answers.

c   Listen to the song again. Then discuss these questions in groups.

1   The singer is addressing a woman. How does she feel at the moment?

2   What does the singer want her to do about her feelings?

3   How does he think he can help?

Private emotion

Every endless (1) ▦ .... has a (2) 🌄 .... day
Every darkest sky has a shining (3) 🔦 ....
And it shines on you (4) 🏃 ...., can't you see
You're the only one who can shine for me?

It's a private emotion that fills you tonight
And a silence falls between us
As the (5) 🗡 .... steal the light
And wherever you may find it, wherever it may lead
Let your private emotion come to me, come to me

When your soul is tired and your (6) ♡ .... is weak
Do you think of love as a (7) ◉ .... street?
Well it runs both ways, open up your (8) 👀 ....
Can't you see me here, how can you deny?

It's a private emotion that fills you tonight
And a silence falls between us
As the (9) 🗡 .... steal the light
And wherever you may find it, wherever it may lead
Let your private emotion come to me, come to me

Every endless (10) ▦ .... has a (11) 🌄 .... day
Every darkest sky has a shining (12) 🔦 ....
It takes a lot to (13) 🙂 .... as your tears go by
But you can find me here till your (14) 😔 .... run dry

3 Speaking

Ricky Martin has become one of the biggest international stars with fans and fan clubs all over the world. In pairs, discuss these questions about fans and fame.

1 Have you ever joined a fan club?
2 Have you ever looked for information about pop or movie stars on the Internet?
3 Have you ever asked a famous person for his / her autograph?
4 Have you ever written a "fan letter?"
5 Have you ever daydreamed about being famous?
6 Do you lose interest in singers or groups when they become too famous?
7 Do you think that famous people should be protected from journalists and photographers?
8 Do you think that the worldwide success of singers like Ricky Martin, from a small island in the Caribbean, helps to create more respect and understanding?

Songsheet 3
When a man loves a woman

1 Word builder: sayings about love

a There are a lot of sayings about love. Look at these eight sayings and put each one into the correct column of the chart below.

Love is inconstant.

For love will man kill.

True love is selfless.

Love makes a fool out of a wise man.

Love liberates.

Love is blind.

Love is knowledge, and knowledge love.

With love everything can be done.

Negative views of love	Positive views of love
Love is inconstant.	

b In pairs, write any other sayings about love that you have heard. Underline the two sayings that you most agree with then discuss your views about love with your partner.

2 Speaking

a Complete these two sentences with ideas of your own.

1 When a man loves a woman, he …   2 When a woman loves a man, she …

b In groups, discuss your sentences.

3 Listening and speaking

a Listen to this song. Is the singer's opinion of love mainly positive or negative? Make notes while you listen to justify your answer. Think about the following.

● type of music   ● singer's voice   ● speed of song   ● lyrics of song

b Now read the lyrics. Underline all the effects that love can have on a man, according to the singer. Then write the effects in your own words, as in the example.

When a man loves a woman, he'd trade the world for the good thing he's found.

When a man loves a woman, he'd give anything to keep the love he's found.

c Listen to the song again while you read the lyrics a second time. Is the man singing about men in general or about his own personal experiences?

When a man loves a woman

When a man loves a woman
Can't keep his mind on nothin' else
He'd trade the world for the good thing
he's found
If she's bad, he can't see it
She can do no wrong
Turn his back on his best friend, if he puts
her down

When a man loves a woman
He'll spend his very last dime
Tryin' to hold on to what he needs
He'd give up all of his comforts
And sleep out in the rain
If she said that's the way it ought to be

When a man loves a woman
I give you everything I have
Tryin' to hold on to your precious love
Baby, please don't treat me bad

When a man loves a woman
Deep down in his soul
She can bring him such misery
If she's playin' him for a fool
He's the last one to know
Lovin' eyes can never see

When a man loves a woman
He can do her no wrong
He can never hold some other girl
Yes, when a man loves a woman
I know exactly how he feels
'Cos baby, baby, baby, you're
my world

When a man loves a woman ...

4 Reading and writing

a Read these two letters. Which one was written by the singer of *When a man loves a woman*, do you think?

A

Honey,

How's life with you? For me it's not so good. I'm as sad as a man can be. I never see my old friends any more – just too busy over here! You know, I think about us now and then. I wish we hadn't argued so much.

We would still be together if ..., but the past is the past.

I hope you're enjoying the apartment I gave you. Is the car still working?

Take care,

Marcus

P.S. If you ever get lonely, call. OK?

B

Baby,

I'm writing from Los Angeles. Sorry I left without talking to you first. I had to leave for a couple of days because my head was exploding. You see, friends tell me that you're seeing another guy, but I don't believe them!

I wish you knew how much I love you.

I've given you everything I can, but maybe that's not enough.

Anyway, I hope and pray that everything will be OK.

I'll call in a day or two.

      Your love,

      Marcus

b In pairs, write a short reply to the letter in no more than 60 words.

c Read your letters to the class. Decide on the best reply.

Songsheet 4
The day before you came

1 Word builder: guessing meaning from context

a Try to guess the meaning of the words in *italic* in the following sentences. Tell
your partner your ideas.

1 Have you read today's *editorial* in the paper? It really criticizes the government.

2 There are *heaps* of clothes all over the bedroom floor. Why don't you put them in the closet?

3 The hours really *dragged* while I was waiting for your flight to arrive.

4 The little girl *cuddled* her teddy bear as she listened to her parents arguing.

5 He *rattled* the coins inside the can to encourage us to give him some more.

6 The teacher *frowned* at the student who arrived late for the exam.

7 She *yawned* as her grandfather told his story for the tenth time.

8 "Who was at the bar?" "No one special. The usual *bunch*."

9 Where is that train? It was *due* ten minutes ago!

10 My flight was delayed three hours. I thought I wouldn't *make* the presentation.

b Now match the words with these meanings.

a) the opposite of *smiled*

b) shook in order to make a noise

c) held closely

d) went slowly

e) took an involuntary deep
breath from boredom or tiredness

f) a newspaper column (giving the newspaper's opinions)

g) a group of people

h) piles

i) manage to get to

j) scheduled to arrive

2 Listening

a This song describes a person's typical day from morning until night. Listen and
write down the times of these actions.

1 ....   2 ....   3 ....   4 ....   5 ....   6 ....   7 ....

b In the song the singer doesn't use the past simple to describe the actions.
What verb form does she use? Why? Listen again if you wish.

c Listen again and complete the song.

The day before you came

I must have left my house at eight, because I always do
My train, I'm (1) ...., left the station just when it was due
I must have read the morning paper going into town
And having gotten through the editorial, no (2) .... I must have frowned
I must have made my desk around a quarter after nine
With letters to be read, and heaps of papers waiting to be (3) ....
I must have gone to lunch at half past twelve or so
The usual place, the usual bunch
And still on top of this I'm pretty sure it must have (4) ....
The day before you came

I must have lit my seventh cigarette at half past two
And at the time I never even noticed I was (5) ....
I must have kept on dragging through the business of the day
Without really knowing anything, I hid a part of me away
At five I must have left, there's no (6) .... to the rule
A matter of routine, I've done it ever since I finished school
The train back home again
Undoubtedly I must have read the evening paper then
Oh yes, I'm sure my life was well within its usual (7) ....
The day before you came

I must have opened my front door at eight o'clock or so
And stopped along the way to buy some (8) .... food to go
I'm sure I had my dinner watching something on TV
There's not, I think, a single episode of *Dallas* that I didn't (9) ....
I must have gone to bed around a quarter after ten
I need a lot of sleep, and so I like to be in bed by then
I must have read a while
The latest one by Marilyn French or something in that (10) ....
It's funny, but I had no sense of living without (11) ....
The day before you came

And turning out the light
I must have yawned and cuddled up for yet another night
And rattling on the roof I must have heard the sound of (12) ....
The day before you came

d The singer is quite sure about what she did on that day. She uses the form *must have* + verb and also several expressions to show that she's sure, such as *no doubt*. Can you find any more of these expressions in the song?

3 Speaking

In groups, discuss these questions.

1 Many love songs are written about first meetings. This song is about the day before. How romantic is it? Refer to the words to justify your opinions.

2 The person in the song is a creature of habit – that is, a person who likes to do the same things at the same time every day. To what degree are you a creature of habit? Give examples from your life.

Songsheet 5
Smooth

1 Word builder: the music business

a Match the expressions on the left with the meanings on the right.

1	to get a Grammy Award	**a)**	a company like Sony Music, which signs artists and makes and sells records
2	to record an album	**b)**	to receive a prize from the American music industry
3	a follow-up	**c)**	to begin to play the guitar, piano, etc.
4	to release a record	**d)**	to have a number one best-selling record
5	to top the charts	**e)**	to perform several tracks in a studio
6	a collaboration	**f)**	to perform in different places
7	to go on tour	**g)**	to make a successful record
8	a record label	**h)**	to begin to sell a CD or album
9	to take up an instrument	**i)**	a project that people work on together
10	to have a hit	**j)**	the next record that you make after a previous release

b The words 1-10 in this article about Carlos Santana are in the wrong place. Decide which of the words should go with each number. Notice that the form of the word is sometimes different.

Carlos Santana has been a famous musician since the 1960s and has (1) ~~topped~~ *recorded* several million-selling albums in his career, but the remarkable success of his 1999 album *Supernatural*, his first for his new (2) *collaborations* .... Arista, took many observers by surprise. This album (3) *took up* .... the American charts for months and won nine (4) *tours* ...., including Song of the Year for *Smooth. Maria Maria* was another huge (5) *label* .... from the album. The album featured (6) *follow-up*

.... with a wide range of other artists and became one of the best-selling albums of all time.

Carlos Santana's musical journey goes back to the 1950s in Mexico, where he first (7) *recorded* .... the guitar. His family later moved to the United States, where Carlos developed his love for the blues and his own distinctive style and sound. When his group performed at the famous Woodstock Music Festival in 1969, they made a sensational impact and the group's first album, *Santana*, (8) *hit*

.... in the same year, sold over two million copies. Their 1970 (9) *released* ...., *Abraxas*, was an even greater international success and there have been over 30 other albums since then with a series of (10) *Grammy awards* .... that have taken them around the world several times. His travels have also included numerous charitable projects, including work for his own charity, Milagro, which helps children in need all over the world.

2 Listening

a Listen to the song and choose the correct answers.

1 The situation in the song is:
    a) a moonlit night.   **b)** a hot noon.   **c)** a cool evening.

2 The man feels that the woman is too:
    a) far away.   **b)** cool.   **c)** hot.

3 His basic attitude towards her is that he:
    a) would prefer to forget her.   **b)** feels ashamed of his feelings for her.   **c)** would do anything for her.

b Now listen again and complete the song.

Smooth

Man! It's a hot one
Like seven (1) .... from the midday sun
I hear you (2) .... and the words melt everyone
But you stay so cool
My munequita, my Spanish Harlem (3) ....
You're my reason for (4) ....
The step in my groove

<u>Chorus</u>
And if you say this life ain't good (5) ....
I would give my world to lift you up
I could change my life to better suit your (6) ....
'Cause you're so smooth
And it's just like the (7) .... under the moon
Well, it's the same emotion that I get from you
You got the kind of lovin' that can be so smooth
Give me your heart, make it (8) ....
Or else forget about it

I'll tell you one thing –
If you would leave it would be a (9) .... shame
In every breath and every word
I hear your (10) .... calling me out
Out from the barrio, you hear my (11) .... on your radio
You feel the turning of the world so soft and (12) ....
Turning you round and round

Repeat chorus

c Now look at the questions in exercise 2a again and check if you were right.

3 Speaking

Carlos Santana is an artist who has been playing and producing successful music for five decades now. Discuss these questions.

1 Do you know any other artists who have achieved this?
2 Do you think it is possible for many artists to continue for so long and to attract younger fans as they get older? Why or why not?
3 Do you feel that older artists should make way for younger artists with different styles?

4 Writing and speaking

Using the vocabulary from exercises 1 and 2, write a short article about an artist you admire and give a presentation, with a piece of their music in the next lesson.

Songsheet 6
Simply the best

1 Word builder: the music business

Complete this short article about Tina Turner, using some of the
words you studied for the song article about Carlos Santana.
The first letter of each missing word is given to help you.

Tina Turner has had a long and varied career in the
music business. Born Anna Mae Bullock in a small,
quiet town in Tennessee, it was her future husband Ike
who gave her the name by which she was to become
famous. She had her first (1) h..................... in 1960 with
A fool in love and went on numerous (2) t.....................
with her husband during the following 15 years. She
(3) t..................... up acting in the 1970s, appearing in the
rock opera *Tommy* and later in *Mad Max 2*.

She left Ike in 1975 and launched her solo career.
Her first album was not a big success, but she changed
to a new (4) l....................., Capitol, and in 1984
(5) r..................... her (6) f..................... album, *Private Dancer*, in London
in only two weeks. It was with one of the songs from the album, *What's
love got to do with it?*, that she finally (7) t..................... the American
charts, and in the same year she won three
(8) G.....................

Since then she has continued to perform and (9) r..................... albums
every few years. Her (10) c..................... include work with Bryan
Adams, Rod Stewart and Mick Jagger, and her autobiography was
turned into a successful movie. Now in her sixties, she is still
considered one of the most charismatic singers in the world.

2 Listening

a These pictures represent words in the song. Listen to the song and number
them in the order you hear them.

b Now listen again and complete the song.

Simply the best

I call you when I (1) .... you. My heart's on fire

You come to me, come to me, wild and wired

Oh, you come to me. Give me everything I need

Give me a lifetime of (2) .... and a world of dreams

Speak the language of love like you know what it (3) ....

Oh, and it can't be (4) ....

Take my heart and make it strong

Chorus

You're simply the best, better than all the (5) ....

Better than anyone, anyone I ever (6) ....

I'm (7) .... on your heart. I hang on every (8) .... you say

Tear us apart, baby, I would rather be (9) ....

In your heart I see the stars every night and every day

In your eyes I get lost, I get (10) .... away

Just as long as I'm here in your arms

I could be in no better (11) ....

Repeat chorus

Each time you leave me I start (12) .... control

You're walking away with my heart and my (13) ....

I can feel you even when I'm (14) ....

Oh baby, never go

Repeat chorus

3 Speaking

In pairs, talk to your partner and try to agree on the best of all the things below.

the best pizza in your town   the best pet to have

the best song in this book   the best place to go shopping

the best way to learn English   the best sport if you want to keep fit

the best advertisement on TV   the best beach near your city

Irregular verbs

Infinitive	Past	Past participle	Unit and lesson
be	was / were	been	U1, L1
become	became	become	U1, L2
begin	began	begun	U1, L3
bite	bit	bitten	U9, L3
break	broke	broken	U1, L2
bring	brought	brought	U2, L1
broadcast	broadcast	broadcast	U3, L1
build	built	built	U6, L3
burst	burst	burst	U9, L3
buy	bought	bought	U2, L1
can	could	could	U1, L1
catch	caught	caught	LC5
choose	chose	chosen	U1, L2
come	came	come	U2, L1
cost	cost	cost	U3, L1
cut	cut	cut	U4, L1
do	did	done	U2, L4
draw	drew	drawn	U8, L2
drink	drank	drunk	U10, L3
drive	drove	driven	U2, L1
eat	ate	eaten	U3, L2
fall	fell	fallen	LC 4
feel	felt	felt	U1, L2
fight	fought	fought	U1, L3
find	found	found	U1, L4
fly	flew	flown	U2, L1
forbid	forbade	forbidden	U10, L3
forget	forgot	forgotten	U2, L3
get	got	gotten	U1, L2
give	gave	given	U1, L4
go	went	gone	U1, L3
grow	grew	grown	U3, L4
hang	hung	hung	U5, L2
have	had	had	U1, L2
hear	heard	heard	U1, L1
hit	hit	hit	U7, L1
hold	held	held	LC2
keep	kept	kept	LC1
know	knew	known	U1, L1
lay	laid	laid	U2, L1

Infinitive	Past	Past participle	Unit and lesson
lead	led	led	U1, L3
leave	left	left	U1, L2
lend	lent	lent	U3, L4
let	let	let	U4, L3
lose	lost	lost	LC1
make	made	made	U1, L2
mean	meant	meant	U3, L3
meet	met	met	U1, L3
pay	paid	paid	U4, L3
put	put	put	U1, L4
read	read	read	U1, L4
ride	rode	ridden	U5, L2
rise	rose	risen	U3, L4
run	ran	run	U2, L3
say	said	said	U1, L1
see	saw	seen	U1, L2
seek	sought	sought	U8, L1
sell	sold	sold	U3, L1
send	sent	sent	LC2
set	set	set	U1, L3
shake	shook	shaken	U4, L3
show	showed	shown	U1, L2
sing	sang	sung	U5, L1
sit	sat	sat	U5, L3
speak	spoke	spoken	U4, L4
spend	spent	spent	U1, L3
spill	spilt	spilt	U9, L1
stand	stood	stood	U2, L2
stick	stuck	stuck	U6, L2
strike	struck	struck	U9, L1
take	took	taken	U2, L1
tell	told	told	LC1
think	thought	thought	U1, L1
throw	threw	thrown	U7, L1
wake	woke	woken	U2, L3
wear	wore	worn	U5, L1
win	won	won	U7, L1
write	wrote	written	U1, L4
understand	understood	understood	U1, L4

Pronunciation chart

Vowels

/i/	eat
/ɪ/	sit
/eɪ/	wait
/e/	get
/æ/	hat
/aɪ/	write
/ʌ/	but
/uː/	food
/ʊ/	good
/oʊ/	go
/ɔː/	saw
/a/	hot
/aʊ/	cow
/ɔɪ/	boy
/iər/	here
/ər/	her
/eər/	hair
/or/	or
/ar/	far

Consonants
(shown as initial sounds)

/b/	bat
/k/	cat
/tʃ/	chair
/d/	dog
/f/	fat
/g/	girl
/h/	hat
/dʒ/	July
/k/	coat
/l/	like
/m/	man
/n/	new
/p/	pet
/kw/	queen
/r/	run
/s/	see
/ʃ/	shirt
/t/	talk
/ð/	the
/θ/	thin
/v/	voice
/w/	where
/j/	you
/ŋ/	sing (as final sound)
/z/	zoo

The alphabet

/eɪ/	/i/	/e/	/aɪ/	/oʊ/	/uː/	/ar/
Aa	Bb	Ff	Ii	Oo	Qq	Rr
Hh	Cc	Ll	Yy		Uu	
Jj	Dd	Mm			Ww	
Kk	Ee	Nn				
	Gg	Ss				
	Pp	Xx				
	Tt					
	Vv					
	Zz					

Macmillan Education
Between Towns Road, Oxford OX4 3PP
A division of Macmillan Publishers Limited
Companies and representatives throughout the world

ISBN 978 0 333 92760 1

Text © Simon Brewster, Paul Davies, Mickey Rogers 2002
Design and illustration © Macmillan Publishers Limited 2002

Songsheets written by Martin McMorrow

First published 2002

Designed by Lodestone Publishing Limited (design: Mind's Eye Design, based on
original design by Kevin Mcgeoghegan)
Illustrated by Chris Forsey, Maureen Gray, Roger Walker, Andy Warrington,
Geoff Waterhouse
Cover design by Katie Austin
Cover photo by Stone

Among all the people who contributed to the Skyline project, the authors give
special thanks to John Waterman and Lucy Torres, who did much more than their
duty as editors. Thank you, John and Lucy! The authors would also like to thank
Katie Austin for the cover design.

The publishers would like to thank the following for reading material and making
comments on books four and / or five: María Luiza de Angeli, ESL Teacher,
Development of special materials, Colegio Santo Americo, São Paulo, Brazil; Vládia
María Cabral Borges, Professor of English Linguistics and Applied Linguistics,
Head of Department of Foreign Languages, University of Ceará, Forteleza, Brazil;
Lueli Loivos Ceruti, Director of Studies, RLC Schools, Brazil; Heriberto Diaz, Head
of the Language Department, Centro de Investigación y Docencia Económicas,
Mexico; Norma Duarte Martinez, English Coordinator, Veterinary Medicine and
Husbandry College, National Autonomous University of Mexico, Mexico D.F.
Mexico; Albina Escobar, Freelance Teacher Trainer and Consultant, Brazil;
Consuelo F. B. Ivo, Supervisor, Centro Cultural Brasil Estados Unidos Campinas,
Brazil; Connie R. Johnson, Co-ordinator of EFL Basic 1 and EFL Professor in the
Language Department, Universidad de las Américas Puebla, México; Carlos
Meléndez, Tecnologico de Monterrey Campus Guadalajara, Mexico; JoAnn Miller,
English Language Academic Coordinator, Universidad del Valle de México, A.C.,
Mexico; Joacyr T. Oliveira, Executive Coordinator, União Cultural Brasil Estados
Unidos, São Paulo, Brazil; Jorge Adolfo Obregon Aragon, English Coordinator,
Instituto Chapultepec A.C., Culiacan, Mexico; Ane Cibele Palma, Academic
Coordinator, Centro Cultural Brasil Estados Unidos Curitiba, Inter Americano-
Curitiba, Brazil; Kathryn Laura Sagert, English teacher, Centro de Investigación y
Docencia Económicas, Mexico.

The publishers gratefully acknowledge the following for permission to reproduce
copyright material: Extract from When cars drive you by Keith Naughton from
Newsweek, 27th December, 1999 © 1999 Newsweek, Inc. All rights reserved.
Reprinted with permission; Extract from Freedom to box by N Warburton: Journal
of Medical Ethics © 1998; 24(1):56-60. Reprinted with permission of BMJ
Publishing Group; Extract from Stars' Salaries: Swish! Time 29th July, 1996. ©
1996 Time Inc. Reprinted with permission; Extract from Reshaping the World
from Newsweek 16th August 1999 © 1999 Newsweek, Inc. All rights reserved.
Reprinted by permission; Extract from Mir drops into the ocean from The
Telegraph 23rd March 2001 © Telegraph Group Limited (2001). Reprinted with
permission; Extract from It's just bad luck that the 13th is so often a Friday by
Robert Matthews from The Telegraph on Sunday, 8th September 1996 ©
Telegraph Group Limited (1996). Reprinted with permission; Extract advertising
Stop Smiling, Start Kvetching: A 5-Step Guide to Creative Complaining by
Barbara Held, Ph.D. reproduced by permission of the Author and Audenreed
Press, a Division of Biddle Publishing Company. Jacket cover reprinted with
permission of the Author and Nancy Love Agency; Extract from Looking on the
bright side can be bad for you by Philip Delves Broughton from The Telegraph,
16th August 2000 © Telegraph Group Limited (2000). Reprinted with permission;
Extract from BA in urgent flight safety review by Tracy McVeigh and Vanessa
Thorpe from The Observer, 31st December 2000 © The Observer (2000).
Reprinted with permission; Extract from 6 Steps to Successful Career Planning
by Deborah Lapoint from www.suite101.com. Reprinted with permission of
Suite101.com; Instructions for Hasami Shogi game from The Book of Classic
Board Games collected by Sid Sackson and the editors of Klutz © 1991 John
Cassidy. Adapted with permission from Klutz; Tapescript material based on text
from KET The Kentucky Network www.dl.ket.org. Used with permission of Joan
Jahnige; Tapescript material based on How To Overcome Shyness by Art Nefsky
www.nefsky.com. Used with permission of Art Nefsky.

The Day Before you came Words and Music by Benny Andersson & Bjorn
Ulvaeus © 1982 Union Songs AB, Stockholm, Universal / MCA Music Publishing
Ltd, 77 Fulham Palace Road, London, W6, reprinted by permission of Music Sales
Ltd and Bocu Music Ltd. All Rights Reserved. International Copyright Secured;
Smooth Words and Music by Robert Thomas and Itaal Shur © 1999, Bidnis Inc and
Itaal Shur Music / EMI Blackwood Music Inc / Writers Designee, USA, reprinted by
permission of EMI Music Publishing Ltd, London WC2H 0QY and International
Music Publications Ltd. All rights reserved; Simply the best Words and Music by
Holly Knight and Mike Chapman © 1988 Knighty Knight Music, administered by
Wixen Music Publishing, Inc and Mike Chapman Enterprises, c/o Zomba Music,
reprinted by permission of I Q Music Ltd.

Every effort has been made to trace copyright holders, but in some cases this has
proved impossible. The publishers would be happy to hear from any copyright
holder that has not been acknowledged.

Picture research by Lodestone Publishing Limited

The authors and publishers would like to thank the following for permission to
reproduce their photographs: AKG pp6(B), 10(A), 93(t); Associated Press
pp8(B), 10(b)(Jantilal), 14(Srakocic), 54(Miller), 65(l)(Lederhandler),
65(c)(Chiasson), 88(B)(Wrighthouse), 97(t)(Advanced Cell Technology);
Bridgeman Art Library p6 (b) (© Succession Picasso/DACS 2000); Candy Express
31; Chris Honeywell p24(T-shirt, trainers); Corbis pp19, 68(B); Eye Ubiquitous
pp10(D)(Page), 56(l)(Skjold), 60(C)(Tornegro), 61(Aidan), 68(C)(Seheult),
85(Seheult), 88((A)(Waterlow), 91(Page); FPG P118; Genesis pp6(t)(NASA),
8(A)(NASA), 79(b)(NASA); Haddon Davies p24(hat, sunglasses, watch); Impact
pp49(t)(Cavendish), 74(r)(Henley); James Davis Worldwide p48; John Walmsley
pp38(tr, bl), 55(2, 4, 5); Kobal p50(l)(The Ladd Company/Warner Brothers),
50(r)(Warner Brothers); Mary Evans Picture Library pp46(b), 74(l); Moviestore
pp6(A)(Miramax), 6(C)(United Artists), 6(D), 70(A); PA pp21(SEPA),
32(Dempsey), 43, 84, 86, 88(C), 98, 101(Butler), 110(Batchelor), 114, 116, 123;
Popperfoto pp9(Reuters), 10(B), 46(t), 56(r)(Gonzales), 62(Mircouch),
65(r)(Josek), 66(t)(Reuters), 66(b), 97(b)(Mitchell); Powerstock/Zefa pp60(A),
100(r), 102((t); Redferns p124(Costello); Rex Features pp10(C), 30(bl),
52(Hibbert), 65(b)(Brown), 68(E); Ronald Grant pp28(t)(Dreamworks/UIP),
28(b), 42(t), 51(United Artists); Ruth Lambert pp99, 102(b); Sally & Richard
Greenhill pp55(1), 60(B)(Greenhill); South American Pictures p49(bl)(Morrison);
Stone pp119, 121, 122; Sylvia Cordaiy pp68(D)(Parker), 100(tl)(Peart),
100(b)(Smith); Telegraph Colour Library pp30(tr)(Taylor), 30(br)(Cuthbert),
36(Rowell), 42(b), 47(l)(Vega), 47(r)(Bibikow), 68(A), 68(F)(Bray),
70(B)(Simpson), 79(t); Tografox pp24(b), 38(tl), 49(r), 55(3), 88(b), 93(b);
Torres p39; Travel Ink pp30(tl)(Reddy); 55(6)(Coyne).

Printed in Thailand

2012 2011 2010 2009 2008
11 10 9 8 7